Legal Almanac Series No. 75

LAWS GOVERNING BANKS AND THEIR CUSTOMERS

by Sidney Mandell

1975 OCEANA PUBLICATIONS, INC.
Dobbs Ferry, New York

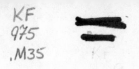
This is the seventy-fifth number in a series of LEGAL
ALMANACS which bring you the law on various subjects
in nontechnical language. These books do not take the
place of your attorney's advice, but they can introduce
you to your legal rights and responsibilities.

Library of Congress Cataloging in Publication Data

Mandell, Sidney, 1904-
  Laws governing banks and their customers

  (Legal almanac series ; 75)
  Includes index.
  1. Banking law--United States. I. Title.
KF975.M35   346'.73'082   75-16311
ISBN 0-379-11100-4

Manufactured in the United States of America

TABLE OF CONTENTS

TO SONIA

FOREWORD

A person who enters a bank to engage in a money transaction is aware that his dealings are circumscribed by a host of rulings established by law and custom. Rarely does he question the bank's interpretation of these regulations even if his negotiations do not turn out as satisfactorily as he expected. Balancing his checkbook is enough of a headache. Besides, he knows he is confronted with an organization whose political and financial clout is considerably stronger than his. Wright Patman, former chairman of the House Banking and Currency Committee, has pointed out that half the deposits of the more than 13,500 commercial banks **strategically** scattered across the fifty states of our land are controlled by fifty institutions - roughly three-tenths of one percent of all the banks in the country. Through one means or another commercial banks now control well over $900 billion, a few deposits short of a trillion.

Control of money and credit by these financial giants affects everyone. The ability to lend or not to lend, to foreclose a mortgage or call in a loan may mean the difference between success or failure to any individual or corporation. It is an awesome power that banks have clung to in spite of efforts to modify it. The banker tends to allocate his funds to fields that will do him the most good. These are not necessarily the areas where they are most needed. Housing, for instance, suffers from a devastating lack of money today but business loans pay banks more. Many economists who see banks as quasi-public institutions clamor for the adoption of a policy of credit allocation by the Federal Reserve Board which after all siphons loan money to banks at bargain rates.

Obviously, the ordinary citizen must utilize banks unless he wishes to hide his cash under the sofa, an inconvenient, unrewarding, and dangerous practice today. He needs banks as much as they need him. However, his use of them can be enhanced if he views them in perspective. Tracing the development of the modern bank sheds light on how effectively both banking and government have answered some of his problems. Understanding the powers and limitations imposed by law on banks enables him to avail himself of their services more wisely. Awareness of the legal pitfalls he may encounter sharpens his perceptions of his own rights and responsibilities. Above all, such knowledge may make him realize he has a genuine stake in helping banks to fulfill the public trust intrinsic in the nature of their business.

Chapter 1

BANKING HISTORY IN THE UNITED STATES

Early Banking

The early American colonists suffered severely from lack of ready money. Throughout most of the eighteenth century, the colonies met the problem by authorizing banks whose sole function was to print batches of paper money to lend against mortgages on land. Merchants made short-term loans secured by goods that they expected to sell and liquidated them at the completion of the sale. It was not until 1781 that Robert Morris, burdened with the task of paying for the Revolutionary War, founded the Bank of North America with funds obtained mostly from abroad. This institution like a modern "checkbook" bank could make short-term loans, accept deposits and deal in bills of exchange. Credit was extended mostly through circulating bank notes and not, as at present, through accumulating deposits.

Ten years later, after the formation of the new federal government, the functions of the Bank of North America as fiscal agent of that government were taken over by the Congressionally chartered First Bank of the U.S., the brainchild of Alexander Hamilton, who envisioned the rapid industrial and commercial growth of the new nation. With its main office in Philadelphia and branches in the leading cities of the country, the bank with a total capital of $10 million, one-fifth subscribed by the federal government, served as a fiscal agent, a source of loanable funds, as well as a bank of note issue and discount. In spite of the vigorous opposition of agrarian-minded Thomas Jefferson, who feared the bank would encourage get-rich-quick speculation, the bank weathered without mishap the twenty years of its charter, which expired in 1811. It had stabilized the currency and adequately controlled credit by its efficient collection of funds due the government.

Meanwhile New York, Massachusetts, and other states had begun to charter banks by special acts of their legislatures. All these were banks of issue. There were no minimum reserve requirements and the bank notes were secured by the general assets of the bank. In addition to lending their credit in the form

1

of notes, these banks accepted deposits and began to lend money to farmers, manufacturers, and others who wanted long-term credit for noncommercial purposes. Well-managed and helped through difficulties by the U.S. Treasury and the Bank of the U.S., many of these banks remained solvent. However, rural banks with fewer outlets for their loans had more difficult sledding than those in cities. In some states that banned note circulation, "private" banks owned by individuals spurned corporate charters and circulated their own notes.

The greatest menace to sound banking was self-serving individuals like the Boston financier Andrew Dexter, who after buying the equities of the Farmers' Exchange Bank of Gloucester, Rhode Island, paid the sellers off with the assets of the bank and became its largest borrower on terms made exclusively by himself. His issuance of $800,000 in bank notes backed by a capital of $45 set a pattern that others were not slow to follow. After the collapse of his bank in 1819, commercial banks for a variety of reasons experienced acute disasters periodically throughout the nineteenth century. Excessive issue of unredeemable paper by the rapidly expanding numbers of state banks during the War of 1812 led to a ruinous inflation in which bank failure became common and people became skeptical of the value of all bank notes whereever issued.

In 1816, Congress, against the opposition of state banks anxious to hold on to the growing deposits of the federal government, was reluctantly forced to charter a Second Bank of the U.S. Under the aggressive direction of Nicholas Biddle, the bank used its power to expand or contract the money market to bring state banks to heel. However, critics of the bank were legion--hard-money agrarians who disliked federal control, state banks that resented competition, businessmen whose requests for loans were turned down, debtor groups that wanted easier money, and those who thought the bank undemocratic and unconstitutional. All these had a powerful spokesman in Andrew Jackson. President Jackson denounced the bank as an odious monopoly operating "to make the rich richer and the potent more powerful." The outcome of the struggle between Biddle and the president was inevitable. Jackson removed the funds of the bank to his "pet" state banks and vetoed the bill extending the charter of the Second Bank. Its life as a federal agency ended in 1836.

The Era of State Banks

The federal government withdrew entirely from any direct

2

dealing with banks. Its new independent treasury scheme provided that all collections due to it were to be paid in specie and stored in its own subtreasury vaults. The responsibility for banking control shifted to the states. Some like South Carolina created their own central bank. Others followed the pattern of New York's free banking system set up in 1838. Anyone could procure a banking charter, but bank notes could only be issued if they were secured by government bonds and reserves held against deposits. No matter which scheme was used, bank failures continued at an alarming rate and a vast variety of state bank notes flooded the country. By the outbreak of the Civil War there were 1600 different state banks issuing 7,000 different currencies. Many could be redeemed when presented at the issuing bank only by a threat of force. Counterfeiting was a thriving business. Depositors and note holders suffered huge losses. At one point during the Civil War the federal government had to turn to a private financier, Jay Cooke, to market its war bonds. The issuing of $450 million in treasury notes unsupported by gold fizzled in 1862 as the "greenbacks" fell in value to 39 cents on the gold dollar.

The National Bank Act

Made desperate by these conditions and harrassed by the ever-pressing need to finance the war, President Lincoln's secretary of the treasury, Salmon P. Chase, persuaded Congress to pass the National Bank Act in 1863. The act provided for a system of national banks established in local communities through the issuing of national charters. It created a uniform national currency by allowing each bank to circulate a limited amount of national bank notes backed by government bonds and redeemable at full value at every other national bank.

Each bank had to maintain a specified reserve of lawful money against its deposits. A comptroller of the currency was appointed to regulate the type and amount of credit expended by the banks. To discourage counterfeiting the government printed notes difficult to reproduce and organized a Secret Service to track down counterfeiters. The first national bank was established at Philadelphia by Jay Cooke on June 20, 1863, followed by some 450 banks that year, of which one-third constituted former state banks. Two years later Congress placed a ten percent tax on new state bank notes, which were thus driven out of circulation. By 1866, nationally chartered banks increased to more than 1600 in number and accounted for more than seventy-five percent of all bank deposits.

A Dual System

The restoration of confidence in the currency diminished runs on banks but their incapacity to go beyond the limits of their own resources restricted the help they could offer to those who needed it. They had difficulty in adapting to seasonal variations in demand for currency. Cash reserves kept in Eastern banks for greater interest were not always available to interior country banks at harvest time. Since there was no central system for interregional check clearance, and long-term loans were beyond the resources of many banks, financing reconstruction in the South or migration to the West was curtailed. There simply was no unified way of channeling funds from the North into the credit-starved sections of the country.

It was easy for the farmers in these regions to blame the national system for their misfortunes and place their confidence in local, state-chartered banks which extended credit to them. These banks developed checking accounts to make up for the loss of state bank notes. The accounts became a major source of deposits and loanable funds so that the number of state banks increased from 2000 in 1866 to 27,000 in 1913. National banks confined themselves more and more to large financial centers where they could supply credit to the vast industrial empire developing in the Gilded Age after the Civil War. Thus a dual banking system of state and national banks became standard for the United States.

Neither system, however, seemed capable of forestalling panics, the most severe of which occurred in the latter part of the nineteenth century at almost regular ten-year intervals. Characterized by runs on banks, due most often to the inability of money-centered banks to recover loans from stockbrokers and investment bankers when stocks fell precipitously, the panics led to widespread suffering and despair. In 1907, the most frightening panic of all up to that time took place. It was severe enough to produce a shortage in the money supply as bank payments stopped everywhere. The panic revealed flaws in the currency and credit structure, which led to the emergency passage of the Aldrich-Vreeland Act authorizing national banks for a period of six years to issue circulating notes based on commercial paper and state, county, and municipal bonds.

4

However, the thoroughly disturbed Congress also added a provision to the act creating the National Monetary Commission to investigate the whole field of banking and currency and recommend needed legislation. The commission's report submitted to Congress in January, 1912, supplemented by the disclosures of the Pujo inquiry of the House Committee on Banking and Currency into the concentration of financial and banking resources, led to the Federal Reserve Act which went into operation in the early fall of 1914, just as war was gripping Europe. The chief intent of Congress was to devise an independent system within the general structure of government that should administer the nation's credit and monetary policies so as to end periodic panics.

Chapter 2

THE FEDERAL RESERVE SYSTEM

Among the chief criticisms leveled at the banking system in the 1912 report presented to Congress by the National Monetary Commission were its inability to mobilize cash reserves in time of need, its difficulty in increasing reserves to meet unusual demands for credit, the inelasticity of its bank notes in meeting varying demands for currency, the inequality of credit facilities in different parts of the country, and the lack of uniform standards for bank regulation and supervision. In many respects the commission's proposals to remedy these defects were similar to those adopted by the Federal Reserve Act. The goals of the act as stated in its title were "to provide for the establishment of Federal Reserve banks, to furnish an elastic currency, to afford means of rediscounting commercial paper, to establish a more effective supervision of banking and for other purposes." It is evident from its operations that the "other purposes" would hopefully include "to foster orderly economic growth, a high level of employment and a relatively stable price level."

Control through the Board of Governors

The Federal Reserve System is a central banking system comprising not one bank, but twelve regional banks, closely coordinated and welded into a single system by a board of governors composed of seven members appointed by the president and confirmed by the Senate. Each governor serves one full term of fourteen years with the terms staggered so that one expires every two years. One of the seven is appointed chairman. The board acts as a policy-making body supervising the entire system. Its principal functions are:

    1. to fix within statutory limits the reserves that member banks are required to maintain against deposit liabilities;

    2. to review and set the discount rate of the Federal Reserve banks;

    3. to participate with the Federal Open Market Committee in determining the terms and conditions under which selective credit controls are to be administered;

4. to determine margin requirements on loans in stock exchange collateral;

5. to set maximum rates payable by banks on time deposits;

6. to supervise Federal Reserve banks and their member banks.

See Appendix B, Items 1, 2, 4, 6, 7. See Appendix G for map.

Federal Reserve Banks

Federal Reserve banks are bankers' banks. They carry out, to a large extent, policies imposed by the board of governors. Located in Boston, New York, Philadelphia, Cleveland, Richmond, Atlanta, Chicago, St. Louis, Minneapolis, Kansas City, Dallas and San Francisco, these banks and their branches deal mostly with the U.S. Treasury and the member banks in their respective districts. Unlike commercial banks they rarely deal with the general public. Most of their activities perform routine services. They participate in policy decisions by proposing changes in the discount rate for final determination by the board and deciding whether or not to make temporary loans to member banks.

An essential part of their work consists of computing the reserve accounts of member banks, which are obliged to carry reserves equal to percentages of their net demand and time deposits. The reserve account balances are also affected by the clearing house postings of the Federal Reserve of paper either drawn upon the member banks or deposited for collection by them. Since all these figures change constantly, the reserve requirements must be retotaled at frequent intervals. Federal Reserve notes, acceptable government obligations, are issued by the Reserve banks to meet seasonal demands for currency. The banks also act as fiscal agents for the U.S. Treasury handling their principal checking accounts as well as the issuing and redeeming of government obligations. A vital service rendered commercial banks is the collection of checks drawn upon banks throughout the country and deposited in localities different from the paying banks. Member and nonmember banks who agree to pay checks without deducting an exchange charge are given this service free.

Each Federal Reserve Bank is a separately incorporated business with a board of nine directors, six of whom are elected by the banks they regulate and three appointed by the board of governors, all serving three-year overlapping terms. Located in the wealthiest city in the world and operating amid the chief money and capital markets, the Federal Reserve Bank of New York occupies a unique place in the system. It is in actual practice a central bank in itself since many of the fiscal operations of the U.S. government as well as the international transactions of the Treasury are conducted in the city. Its foreign exchange division handles not only the accounts of foreign countries but those of large financial bodies like the World Bank and the Bank for International Settlements.

Although Federal Reserve banks are essentially private institutions owned by their member banks, their public nature is readily revealed by the distribution of their net earnings. Dividend payments are limited to the six percent of stock held by member banks and the remainder, after deduction for current needs, is handed over to the Treasury. In 1970, for instance, after deducting $321 million in operating expense and retaining an allowable surplus of $32.5 million, the twelve banks paid out $41 million in dividends to member banks and handed over $3.5 billion to the treasury. (See Appendix B, Items 3 and 5.)

Member Banks

All national banks must join the Federal Reserve system. Qualified state-chartered banks may also become members. Every member bank must subscribe an amount equal to six percent of its own capital and surplus to the capital stock of its district Reserve bank. Only half of its contribution must be paid in immediately, the other half remaining subject to call. Of the nation's 13,634 commercial banks in 1973, 5,737, of which 4,661 were national banks, had become members. They held seventy-seven percent of all the deposits in the country. Many of the smaller state banks will not join the system because they prefer the lower limits of interest-bearing reserves permitted by their states.

Member banks temporarily in need of funds are able to borrow additional reserves from their district banks and to use Reserve facilities for collecting checks, settling clearance balances and transferring funds to other cities. They may also obtain necessary currency and helpful financial information. They are regularly paid their statutory dividend of six percent on their holdings in the district Reserve bank and elect six of the nine directors of their district bank's board of directors. In return, they are expected to comply with reserve requirements bearing no interest and to subject themselves to various federal restrictions. State member banks must permit supervision and examination by the District Reserve bank.

Open Market Committee

Perhaps the most important division of the whole system is the Open Market Committee, composed of the entire board of governors and five presidents of district banks elected annually. Assisted by a staff of experts, this committee at closed meetings formulates policies with respect to the purchase and sale of government securities.

Operations of the System

The banking network is the medium through which the monetary policies of the Federal Reserve are achieved. By regulating the reserve position of member banks, the system exercises control over the volume of banks' deposits and the supply, availability, and cost of credit. The three chief tools used in the process by the board of governors are engaging in open market operations, changing the discount rate, and requiring different reserve ratios. Of these, open market operations, because of their flexibility, are most often used. Such maneuvers have a serious impact on the market prices and yields of government securities, affecting the interest rates in the short-term markets also. The purchases of government securities expand member bank reserve balances, thus giving them more money to lend. Conversely, sales of the securities tighten the money supply and check loans.

Changes in the discount rate, which is the cost of member banks borrowing from the Reserve banks, sometimes signal a shift in monetary policy. More often, however, they are designed to discourage borrowing from the Reserve banks. Variations in the discount rate affect short-term market rates and influence the rates on prime business loans.

Raising or lowering member bank reserve percentages has been used sparingly because of the volume of reserves concerned in such manipulations. Since 1951, when an accord with the Treasury relieved the Federal Reserve from pegging government securities at par, reserve changes have been downward. After 1960, by permitting member banks to count the cash in their vaults as required reserves, the necessity to change the legal reserve requirements has often been averted.

In recent years the structure of the system has been attacked as cumbersome and the secrecy of some of its activities, especially the Open Market Committee, has provoked charges of all kinds of shenanigans. Some find the system too independent of Congress, others too subservient to bankers, and still others as not carrying out the policies of the national government. However, most of the conflict about the Federal Reserve is an outgrowth of the differing views of two schools of economic thought. The "fiscalists," following the views of John Maynard Keynes, popular since the 1930s, seek to regulate what they regard as an essentially unstable economy by changes in government fiscal policy while the "monetarists," influenced by Milton Friedman of the University of Chicago, contend that the economy can be stable if the money supply is controlled.

Monetarists see the Federal Reserve as too concerned with adjusting interest rates and foreign exchange while neglecting the money supply. Far from stabilizing the economy, the Reserve, they maintain, has simply seesawed it by abruptly adding or subtracting money whose purchasing power is "unreal" at various times. Furthermore, it goes off on too many tangents, helping the Treasury raise money for a particular corporation in trouble, like the Penn Central, when it should be sticking to its chief task--the stabilization of the economy.

The Federal Reserve system is not unmindful of the criticism, but it insists that the money supply needs managing if it is to grow and that its policies do that in effect. It is also aware that changes in the interest rate ceilings seem only to have shifted money from one source to another and has tried to modify its policy. Nevertheless, although still working on the assumption that changing interest rates can influence investment and consumer spending enough to control the rate of growth of the money supply, the Reserve has been forced to examine that assumption more closely because of soaring inflation and threats of recession. As a result it has been paying increased attention to other factors affecting the money supply.

Chapter 3

AFTER THE FED

Collapse

Since the inception of the Federal Reserve system, the course of commercial banking has been closely linked to its operation and development. The Fed's excellent job in helping to finance World War I may have led inadvertently to the over-reliance on its powers that triggered the failures, between 1921 and 1934, of numerous inadequately capitalized, poorly managed, state banks reluctant to join the new system. By 1929, over 5,000 banks had suspended operations. Most of these took place in the depressed agricultural sections of the country, but intense competition also led larger banks to swallow smaller ones in urban centers. The stock market crash with its resultant unprecedented declines in values and business activity continued the stream of failures. The situation reached such proportions by March, 1933, that President Franklin D. Roosevelt closed all banks for a four-day "bank holiday." The international monetary and credit mechanism had simply collapsed.

Recovery

Within two months, strenuous measures enabled 12,000 banks with ninety percent of the nation's bank deposits to be back in business. Recovery was sparked by the Emergency Banking Act of March 9, 1933, which provided enough capital to reopen the banks and assure adequate currency to meet all demands in the form of Federal Reserve Bank Notes without gold backing. The Glass-Steagall Banking Act of June, 1933, creating the Federal Bank Deposit Insurance Corporation dispelled the small depositor's fear of loss. Out of its capital of $150 million the FDIC was authorized to guarantee bank deposits up to $5,000 per depositor (now $40,000). The bill also extended open market activities of the Federal Reserve Bank to enable it to prevent excessive speculation on credit, permitted branch banking and widened the Reserve system to include savings and industrial banks. Most controversial of its provisions was its prohibition of interest payments on demand deposits to dampen competition among banks for deposits. Defense spending in the late thirties, placing greater requests for money on the banking system, accelerated its recovery.

After the War

During World War II, commercial and Federal Reserve banks purchased $100 billion in government securities which became the largest proportion of bank assets. In recent years a shift from federal to state and municipal obligations has occurred. Since 1945, the massive increase in industrial population, as well as the so-called population explosion, has accentuated the need for banking services everywhere. Banks have become the "variety stores" of the financial business, offering a diverse array of loans and services. Perhaps the most significant change in American banking since the twenties has been in the quality of bank assets, whose emphasis has shifted from short-term commercial lending to investment in government securities and long-term lending to business, homeowners, consumers, and others.

All of this has necessitated a vast expansion of banking facilities and services. By 1974, the 14,117 commercial banks in the U.S.A. had 26,251 branches, 2,000 of which opened in 1973 alone. The growth of branch banking indicated that the trend toward concentration initiated in the twenties still prevailed. (See Appendix C, Item 4.)

Multiple Banking

The impact of the banking crisis in the early thirties led authorities, both state and national, to approve of banks opening branches as substitutes for an immoderate number of small unit banks. Multiple-office banking in the form of branch or group banking expanded. Group banking grew out of using the holding company device to control the operations of several banks, as in the case of the Giannini family and their Bank of America.

Branch banking poses the question as to whether or not the diversification of assets and economies gained by branching are worth the loss of that responsiveness to local needs characteristic of the unit bank. More efficient management of branch banks does not necessarily mean more effective management in

12

accomplishing the bank's goals. The more than 7,000 members of the Independent Bankers' Association of America maintain that the concentration of power by a few vast institutions threatens the stability of our economy. They lobby vigorously against branch banking and bank holding companies.

State laws concerning branching and holding companies differ widely since many states are anxious to protect banks already entrenched within their borders. Up to 1973, fifteen states prohibited banks from opening branches under any circumstances and fifteen more restricted branching only to local markets. Group banking has been used especially in states that prohibit branch banking. In New York, bank holding companies have been permitted to function statewide and large banks like Chase Manhattan and First National City have been using this stratagem to open or buy up subsidiary banks, especially on Long Island. By 1976, commercial banks as well as mutual savings banks and savings and loan associations will be able to establish branch offices and merge with other banks anywhere in New York with the approval of the regulatory agencies.

Bank Holding Companies

Perhaps the most controversial move toward bank concentration has been the one-bank holding company. Bank mergers restricting competition had been more or less effectively stifled by the Bank Merger Act of 1966 and the legal activities of the Department of Justice under section 7 of the Clayton Anti-Trust Act. The Bank Holding Company Act of 1956 required any corporation owning twenty-five percent or more of the voting stock of two or more banks to register with the Board of Governors of the Federal Reserve. The act further demanded that bank holding companies divest themselves of control of all nonbanking or non-bank-related corporations. However, the act created a wide loophole by exempting those holding companies with only one bank from registering. Major banks interested in business other than banking began to take advantage of the one-bank exemption in the late sixties. The first of these was the First National City Bank, which was followed, by the end of 1968, by thirty-four of the largest commercial banks in the U.S.A. In effect each one of these holding companies created a conglomerate with its own bank to finance nonbanking activities. Fears stemming from the increased power of these giants led Congress to close the one-bank escape hatch in 1970 by restricting these holding companies

13

to acquiring businesses only closely related to banking and giving the Federal Reserve power to determine permissible acquisitions.

However, bank holding companies have continued to expand. They have been allowed to enter into fields ranging from data processing to investment banking. By 1974 their number had increased to almost 1700, controlling over 3000 commercial banks with more than sixty-five percent of all commercial bank deposits. On October 21, 1974, Dr. Arthur Burns, chairman of the Federal Reserve Board, voiced his fears over the adequacy of capital to support such an expansion. In an address to the American Bankers' Association, he complained: "The capital cushion that plays such a large role in maintaining confidence in banks has become thinner primarily because parent holding companies have increased their equity investments in subsidiary banks by using funds raised in the debt market."

Whether or not these colossi are meeting the banking needs of people today is an open question. Strong inflation, accompanied by high interest rates and growing unemployment, has turned attention to the safety of financial institutions. Carl K. Dellmuth, Pennsylvania's secretary of banking, points out that 99.7 percent of all depositors in banks closed in the United States in the years 1934-1973 have recovered every penny of their funds. Critics maintain that banks are too obsessed with earnings growth. Foreign exchange trading losses and questionable real estate loans can only be explained in terms of a quest for growth at any cost. Examples multiply. Excessive trading accounted for a $3.31 million loss by New Jersey's fourth largest bank. Chase Manhattan's president reported that his bank's $800 -million bond trading account should have been valued $34 million lower-- a rectification that wiped out most of Chase's earning increase for the first nine months of 1974. One of the giants, the Franklin National Bank, actually folded up and had to be sold by the FDIC-- a scandal of mammoth proportions.

All these and other manifestations of shaky management have led to serious inquiries as to just what the role of banks in our society should be. One analyst urges banks to simmer down and care less for growth. "Banks weren't created primarily to trade bonds or foreign currency in the first place," he asserts. Another points out that holding companies have diversified far afield on precious little capital. Concerned with such criticism, the Bank of America, the nation's largest bank, whose earnings assets increased sixteen percent in the first part of 1974, decided in October of that year on a formal policy of restraint that will make borrowing from it more difficult and may slow its growth. A.W. Clausen, its president, warned that recent rates of growth could be sustained "only at the risk of eroding future strength and stability." "We are convinced," he emphasized, "that stockholders, depositors and the public are better served by a policy that gives the quality of assets and the stability of earnings higher priority among corporate goals than size alone."

It is obvious that many of the recent calamities have been limited to some of the largest and most expansion-minded banks. An associate editor of Fortune, Peter Vanderwicken, in an article in the New York Times of November 24, 1974, observed that only seventy-eight commercial banks have deposits in the billions and that almost ninety percent of commercial banks have less than $50 million in deposits. "The big banks' troubles," he asserts, "despite the real and grave dangers they pose for the economy, are not common in the country as a whole." His picture of the Quakertown National Bank with deposits of $31.5 million in deposits would seem to bear him out. (See Appendix C, Items 1, 2, 3, and 5.)

It may very well be that banks are entering a stage in which emphasis on size and growth may give way to social need. Some signs of this may be seen in lessened opposition to Congressional proposals for more uniform reserves requirements for banks and greater allocation of money and credit to deprived areas. An alarmed Congress is also tightening controls on large enterprises. In November, 1974, it expanded the Federal Reserve Board's authority to issue cease and desist orders to cover parent holding companies and nonbanking subsidiaries where the actions of either constitute a serious threat to the "safety, soundness or stability" of a subsidiary bank.

Chapter 4

COMMERCIAL BANKS--SERVICES AND REGULATION

Demand and Time Deposits

Banks, as we have seen, are the indispensable sources of money and credit in the world economy. They furnish the bulk of funds as well as the credit mechanism that keeps it circulating. The term "commercial bank" is applied to a lending institution that creates primary demand deposits--bank deposits against which checks can be drawn and credit extended to borrowing customers. Commercial banks embrace a wide variety of institutions including national banks, incorporated state banks, trust companies, private banks, industrial banks specifically authorized to accept deposits, and special types of banks of deposit. They are particularly distinguished from mutual savings banks and savings and loan associations, which accept only time deposits--deposits withdrawable at a specified future date or requiring thirty or more days notice of withdrawal. Savings deposits, for instance, are time deposits of individuals and non-profit organizations that must be evidenced by a passbook. Next to demand deposits, savings accounts are the largest single source of funds for most commercial banks. To eliminate cut-throat competition among banks, the Banking Act of 1933 prohibited interest payments on demand deposits and limited the maximum interest paid on different classes of time and savings deposits.

Primary and Secondary Deposits

Individuals as well as organizations of all types find it convenient to keep money balances as demand deposits with commercial banks. By writing checks, depositors transfer all or part of their account balance to pay for purchases and satisfy debt or other obligations. Their primary deposits supply the bank with new funds to lend or invest. Furthermore, they also originate secondary deposits when the banks make loans. The amount of the loan is simply credited to the borrower's checking account, "creating" a new deposit just as spendable as any the borrower might have put into the bank from his own funds. Thus, each transaction results in increasing demand deposits on the books of the bank. The first results from the actual transfer of money by the customer to the bank; the second from a deposit increase by the bank when it makes a loan.

New Depositors

Although most banks are engaged in a constant struggle for new depositors, some insist on a minimum deposit before accepting would-be customers. These minimums, which vary with the size and location of the bank, often range from $100 to $5,000. A prospective depositor, after an initial interview and acceptance, usually fills out "new account" and "signature" cards. The bank is under no obligation to honor a check in which the depositor's signature deviates from that on the card. Various types of accounts may be opened, including those in the names of two or more persons. Banks require corporations to file a resolution of their directors authorizing the opening of the account and to specify the officers delegated to sign checks and other instruments of payment as well as borrow money and pledge the credit of the corporation. Partnerships must file a copy of the partnership agreement.

Bank Services

Depositors use banks mostly to make deposits and cash checks. Modern banks have tried to make these services as quick and convenient as possible. Magnetic ink numerals on checks, for instance, make possible automated check handling. Signature validation systems now flash the depositor's signature and other data on television-like screens to confirm check-cashing or withdrawal transactions instantly. The commercial bank through its clearing house associations is the only mechanism available to process the ever-mounting volume of commercial paper used today for prompt, efficient collection. A clearing house is merely a meeting place where an association of banks from a particular region engage in the daily exchange of checks, drafts, and other evidences of indebtedness held by one member and due from another. A member bank is credited with its obligations against other banks to whom they are delivered and, in turn, is charged with the obligations of other banks against it and also receives them. A balance is struck and the amount due or owing is determined for each bank. The larger associations are equipped with all sorts of electronic computational devices. The New York Clearing House has an exchange exceeding $1 trillion annually.

To attract and retain customers, banks offer numerous other services and inducements. Checks are more than cash-securing devices. When cancelled by a bank, they are excellent evidence of payment of bills. Periodic balance sheets of his account issued by the bank help the depositor's bookkeeping. Some banks will prepare payrolls and paychecks for businesses. Bank computers are increasingly used to audit the books of firms or help in making tax returns. Most banks are equipped with vaults and safe-deposit boxes rented to customers at small, annual fees. Instruments like cashiers' checks, bank drafts, money orders, travelers' checks and letters of credit are readily available. More and more banks offer advice to customers on an extensive range of business subjects such as pension funds, domestic and foreign markets, security investment possibilities, and estate planning.

Loans

Lending is the lifeblood of a bank. It is the most profitable activity of a commercial bank. Not only does it yield a higher return than investments, but borrowers as a rule keep their deposit balances at their bank and use the other services offered to them. Throughout their history the solvency of banks has depended on the quality of their loans. The mass of a bank's assets is in its loan and discount portfolios. Borrowing is vital to small and medium-sized businesses without access to the capital markets. It is a tremendous aid to enhancing the life of the homeowner and consumer.

Technically, a loan transaction is one where interest is payable either at maturity or periodically over the loan period. On discount loans, interest is deducted in advance from the face of the loan. Demand loans are payable at the call of either party to the loan. Time loans have a definite date of maturity but are often renewable. Loans and discounts may be either unsecured or secured by a pledge of some asset. Bills of lading, for example, are widely used as collateral for loans on commodities in transit since they are required to gain possession of the goods. The most important type of security is usually stocks or bonds.

Kinds of Loans

Loans are generally classified for statistical purposes according to the nature of the borrower or the aim for which the funds are used. A little over one-third are commercial and industrial or business loans, either short-term, with maturities less than a year, or long-term, a year or over. Farm loans aggregate much less in volume. Loans made by banks, intended to be used for the purchase or carrying of securities, customarily demand that the securities be pledged as collateral. Because the government is concerned about the amount of bank credit used for speculation in securities, a national bank may not lend more than ten percent of its unimpaired capital and surplus to one borrower except when the loan is secured by federal government obligations. The Federal Reserve also limits margin requirements to restrict loan amounts. The majority of security loans are made by large metropolitan banks. About seven percent of the loans made today are to finance institutions, other banks, or nonbanking financing companies such as insurance or mortgage companies and saving and loan associations. Indirectly, these loans finance mortgages, consumer loans, and security purchases, and their growth in recent years has been rapid.

Second to business loans in importance are real estate loans, mostly mortgage loans on farms as well as urban property. They pay a high yield in return for slow liquidity.

Congress is at present attempting to curb the practice of "redlining"--the process in which lending institutions refuse to make conventional mortgage or home improvement loans in areas they deem risky, usually older city neighborhoods. This issue has brought community organizations in direct conflict with banking groups at congressional hearings.

Consumer Credit

Although it was not until the end of World War II that commercial banks entered the field of consumer credit, they are now the largest supplier of funds to finance consumer expenditures. Most of these loans are installment credit since almost anything can be bought on a "buy now, pay later" basis. Banks are large buyers of installment contracts from merchants, which often makes them holders in due course and legally exempt from claims as to the quality of the purchased goods--a matter that has caused consumer organizations much concern. Consumer loans have grown so spectacularly that many banks have opened

19

separate departments for handling them and have also gone into the credit card business. (See Appendix E, Items 1, 2, and 3.) By 1970, commercial banks' share of all such lending was forty-two percent.

They have, however, faced a barrage of charges of discrimination in granting loans of this type, accused of secretly denying credit to potential borrowers because of race, sex, type of job, and marital status, among other things. In 1974, the federal government passed an amendment to a Deposit Insurance Bill outlawing discrimination on the basis of sex or marital status. Thirty-three states have laws, of varying efficacy, banning types of loan discrimination. The New York State law enacted in July, 1974, prohibits withholding credit on the basis of sex, marital status, race, creed, color, national origin, age, or childbearing capacity.

Investments

Besides lending money, banks invest in securities to provide themselves with income. A bank's investments include its holdings of home mortgages, bonds, and other long-term credit instruments. Banks usually limit their own investments to direct obligations of the government and federal agencies, tax-exempt obligations of the states and their political subdivisions, and obligations of railroads, public utilities, and industrial companies. Statutory limitations are invariably placed on the holding of any class of these issues except securities of the federal government. Under the Banking Act of 1935, the Comptroller of the Currency sets the standards of investment quality for banks, exempting from his regulations issues of the federal government, of the states and their political subdivisions, and those of a number of specialized banks bearing federal charters, such as federal land banks.

The greater part of a bank's investment portfolio is primarily in government securities because of their safety, relative stability in price, their availability at almost any desired maturity, their acceptability as collateral for loans at Federal Reserve banks, and their security for public deposits. Banks induced by a desire to help their community often buy tax-exempt municipal securities, reserving their smallest use of funds for corporate bonds, notes, and debentures authorized for national banks through the McFadden-Pepper Act of 1927. In addition to buying and selling exempt securities for their own account, national banks act as agents for others in buying stocks and bonds.

Although investment advice for customers is common in most banks, their growing brokerage service has been looked upon askance. In fact, a recent plan of several banks to offer their customers an opportunity to buy stock in small amounts with the cost automatically deducted monthly from their checking account has precipitated a charge that banks are returning to the investment business--an activity presumably forbidden by the Banking Act of 1933. The plan brings into question a wide variety of investment services now looked upon as possible violations-- stock dividend reinvestment plans, individual portfolio management services, investment advisory help and voluntary investment plans. Although the Supreme Court held in 1971 that the management of commingled investments by banks gave rise to the operation of a mutual fund prohibited by the Banking Act, advocates of the new plan maintain it is legal. Vigorously opposed by brokers, the automatic investment service plan faces a show-down that may be resolved by a Congressional review of the whole question.

Increasing the Money Supply

Through lending and investing their surplus funds, commercial banks create a continuous supply of money. Funds flow into the bank through deposits which are then lent and invested, resulting in sufficient assets to pay off the demand deposit liabilities and continue the flow of money into more loans and investments. Changes in the amounts of loans and investments cause corresponding changes in bank deposits. The volume of deposits of member banks in the Federal Reserve system, in turn, affects the amount of legal reserves required of them. Thus, the volume of loans and investments is tied to the sum of reserve balances. For example, if reserve requirements averaged twenty percent of all deposits and member banks equaled five times their reserves, in order to increase their loans and investments, banks would have to obtain additional reserve balances. An additional $1 billion of reserve balances supplied by the Federal Reserve would allow banks to expand their credit as much as $5 billion. Conversely, if the volume of reserve balances should decline, banks would be forced to liquidate loans and investments until deposits had decreased by five times the decrease in the reserve balances. Although only member banks are affected directly by Federal Reserve action, other banks are affected indirectly because they keep their state-required reserves as deposits with member banks.

Trust Business

Taking in deposits and lending out money may be the basic role of a bank, but most growing banks long for a larger part. Trust business offers them the opportunity. Although by law the trust business of a bank is required to be kept entirely separate from its other functions, trust departments may use the facilities of their banks to effect sales and purchases of securities and may open deposits for beneficiaries to receive and hold income from trust accounts. In addition, idle trust funds awaiting investment or distribution may be deposited in special accounts usually required to be secured by collateral. As a result a not inconsiderable income from its trust department flows into the coffers of a commercial bank.

Trust departments handle personal and corporate trusts of all kinds. Their primary function is to conserve private property against waste and loss. The trust company as trustee often takes title to property or manages a business as directed by a trust agreement, a will, or a law. Banks handling personal trusts serve as executors and administrators of estates, trustees under the wills of deceased persons or agreements of deeds of trust, guardians of the property of minors or incompetent persons, and in various fiscal capacities. Corporate trust business may include acting as a trustee under corporate mortgage or reorganization plans or administering the funds of research foundations, hospitals, and religious or educational institutions. As agents, trust companies provide safekeeping and custodial services, hold property in escrow, and act as registrars and agents for corporate securities.

Trust business of necessity is confined only to large banks. In 1968, a staff study of the Domestic Finance subcommittee of the House Committee of Banking and Finance reported that the 3,125 banks empowered to open trust departments held corporate and personal trust assets worth $253.3 billion--forty-one percent of all the assets held by commercial banks. Five banks commanded almost a quarter of this amount. By 1972, the total figure had grown to be more than $343 billion with the Morgan Guarantee controlling more than $23 billion. More reflective of the growing power of business over industry was the disclosure in the 1968 study that 49 banks had representatives on 268 boards of directors of the 500 largest industrial corporations in the United States. Not only were the banks managing trustees of blocks of securities of which their banks were creditors, but they also held numerous interlocking directorates.

Whether or not the spread of banks into other fields is desirable, as bank spokesmen maintain, is still an unresolved question. Among those who believe the public will be better served if banks stick closer to banking is the New York legislature which, in 1973, passed a bill making interlocking directorates illegal among the state's financial institutions.

International Banking

An important factor affecting the nature of commercial banks has been the lightning spread of international banking. Eager to serve their corporate customers abroad, many major banks during the 1960s developed enormous Eurocurrency markets generating funds to support their own domestic business and finance multinational business. United States' banks operate more than 700 foreign branches with total assets of more than $100 billion. First National City Bank derives more than half its income from international activities. At present, more than 125 members of the Federal Reserve system have opened branches in 76 foreign countries and oversea areas of the U.S.A. American banks have sprouted throughout Latin America and the Middle East. Meanwhile more than 60 large foreign bank, totaling assets of $40 billion, have opened banking offices here.

One aspect of this interchange has been to multiply the already large and risky ventures of commercial banks in foreign exchange business. Big commercial banks have always supported a continuous in and out flow of foreign exchange that affects the balances they keep in foreign financial centers. They acquire exchange through interest coupons in foreign currency, drafts, and remittances, as well as foreign currency notes sent overseas, for collection and credit to their own account against their balances abroad. These balances ordinarily do not oscillate much from day to day, but uncertain economic factors plus heavy speculations by dealers, brokers, and some banks have caused sharp rate fluctuations at times, with severe repercussions here and abroad. Arbitrage losses, in which banks and others buy exchange in one market and sell it in another to profit from price differences, may have been partly the cause of the failure of the Franklin National Bank in 1974.

Bank Regulation

From earliest times, alarming experiences with the safety

of banks have caused authorities to be watchful of their operations. Congress and the legislatures of the fifty states have
repeatedly enacted laws to regulate and supervise banking. Nevertheless, Dr. Arthur F. Burns, chairman of the Federal Reserve
Board, has charged that the regulatory system has "failed to
keep pace" with changes in the banking system. The parallel and
sometimes overlapping roles of the Federal Reserve and the
Federal Deposit Insurance Company, he declares, have created
"a jurisdictional tangle that boggles the mind."

Each of the states has at least one agency controlling banks,
and some have special laws for bank holding companies. At the
federal level, every bank whose deposits are insured is subject
to supervision and regulation but authority is divided. The comptroller of currency charters and supervises national banks, controls the reserves as well as operations of all members of the
Federal Reserve and regulates all holding companies. The FDIC
insures most banks but supervises only state-chartered, non-
Reserve members. Complicating this has been the question of
who regulates foreign banks and American banks operating
abroad.

Nevertheless, since 1938, federal agencies have agreed on
uniform procedures and each accepts examiners' reports furnished by the other. The FDIC and the Federal Reserve cooperate
with state supervisory bodies. It is the duty of all examiners to
see that management practices are effective, that all rules and
regulations are observed, that the bank is sound, and that closing
or reorganization is recommended if it is not sound.

The Federal Deposit Insurance Corporation

In spite of the vigilance of all these watchdogs, banks do
fail. To protect depositors as much as possible the FDIC, originally under the Federal Reserve system, has been allowed to
operate under its own steam since 1950. It is managed by a board
of three directors--the comptroller of currency and two presi-
dential appointees. Its early $280-million capital stock furnished
by the government and the Federal Reserve banks has been
retired and replaced by a Deposit Insurance Fund culled from
regular assessments of the insured banks, additions from the
government, and assets formerly held by suspended banks in
process of liquidation. In 1973, the fund aggregated $5.2 billion.
About eighty percent of all commercial banks and seventy percent
of mutual savings banks are now insured by the FDIC. As of

November, 1974, the maximum insurable deposit in one name in one bank is $40,000 while time and savings deposits of public funds of federal, state, and local governments will be insured for $100,000. (See Appendix F, Item 2.) All national banks and state bank members of the Federal Reserve are required to be insured. All nonmember banks may apply by complying with statutory requirements.

The powers of the FDIC are extensive. It has particular jurisdiction over insured banks who are not members of the Federal Reserve system--to examine them regularly, to approve or disapprove of their plans to reduce capital, or to open a branch. It sees that they pay no interest on demand deposits and the legal interest on time and savings deposits. It can also terminate the insured status of any bank that continues after a hearing to engage in unsafe and unsound banking practices. It passes upon all mergers, conversions, and consolidations of insured banks and also acts as a receiver for national and state banks placed in receivership by state authorities. To preserve depositors' funds, the FDIC can make loans to or purchase assets from insured banks. It may facilitate mergers and consolidations to avoid risks or possible loss to itself. Finally, it can prevent the closing of an insured bank and open a closed one to provide adequate banking services in a community.

Limiting Failures

Since the FDIC began operations on January 1, 1934, it has tried to keep the number of closed banks to a minimum. (See Appendix F, Items 1 and 2.) It is proud of the fact that in 1972 it could report only one closing in the country. Although the FDIC chairman, Frank Wille, has warned bankers that "neither the Federal Reserve nor the FDIC is a government charity and we have no intention of protecting poor management against the consequences of incompetence or misconduct," the FDIC has found it possible sometimes to arrange "purchase and assumption" transactions in which another bank takes over a failed bank's deposit liabilities. However, in other cases it has had to pump funds into banks to keep them afloat, and subsequent losses have rarely been negligible. The Sharpstown State Bank of Houston, Texas, for instance, closed its doors on January 25, 1971, after engaging in unusually devious practices, culminating in an FDIC loss estimated to be $24 million.

The FDIC keeps a sharp and continuous eye on its list of

150 "problem" banks--banks that seem to be on the verge of trouble. A survey of fifty-six bank failures made by the FDIC revealed that thirteen banks failed because of loans to its own management, another nineteen not only because of such loans but also of others that obviously should not have been made, while fourteen went down the drain because of embezzlement by their employees. The FBI figures of criminal attacks on federally regulated banks are startling. Total loot during the fiscal year 1974 amounted to almost $20 million (after recoveries), but embezzlement by bank employees took a far greater toll. In 1970, for instance, 4175 embezzlements adding up to $73 million were reported. In the same year, fraud ranging from simple forgery to outright looting totaled three times the $12.6 million plundered by burglars and bandits.

Concern over losses of all kinds has intensified criticism of the regulatory agencies, whose structure Dr. Burns thinks is the most serious obstacle to improving the regulation and supervision of banking. He believes that the present multiagency system may set the stage for competition among regulators "sometimes to relax constraints, sometimes to delay corrective measures." However, there seems to be no general agreement among Federal Reserve or FDIC officials that centralizing regulation is either feasible or necessary.

Chapter 5

SAVINGS BANKS AND SAVINGS AND LOAN ASSOCIATIONS

Savings Bank Development

To many who follow the injunction of Oliver Wendell Holmes to "put not your trust in money but your money in trust," a savings bank is the ideal depository of funds. Essentially, savings banks were founded to offer security to those who suffered from the lack of it--the poor and the laboring class in the community. Very active in the early formation of such banks was the Reverend Henry Duncan of Ruthwell parish in Dumfrieshire, Scotland, where he established a bank in 1810. Six years later the idea spread to the United States with the opening of the Saving Fund Society in Philadelphia and the Provident Institution for Savings in Boston. Both these institutions were chartered by their respective states and are still flourishing today.

The concept on which these organizations was founded is still the basis of mutual savings bank structure--depositors furnish funds and receive the benefit of their use. Possessing no stockholders, the mutual bank distributes all net earnings except for necessary reserves to depositors who have the legal status of creditors. If the institution is liquidated, depositors receive all the assets pro rata after expenses are paid. The depositors have no voice in the operation of the bank, which is managed by a board of trustees, usually the self-perpetuating founders of the bank, who maintain a strictly fiduciary relationship with the organization. Except when they function in a salaried position, they receive no compensation and are prohibited by law from receiving direct or indirect benefits from the actual operation of the bank. The officers of the bank are selected by them.

Regular savings deposits supply the greater part of the bank's funds but a varied number of special savings club accounts are now common. Massachusetts, Connecticut, and New York permit savings banks to offer life insurance and annuities in limited amounts to the public. These policies are increasingly popular among people of limited income, totaling today almost $3 billion in the three states in which they are available. The FDIC insures almost eighty-five percent of the deposits of all mutual savings banks up to the present $40,000 limit. In Massachusetts, banks have retained their own deposit insurance system. Depositors receive interest or dividends whose rates are declared by the trustees, subject at present to the authority of the federal regulatory agencies to set interest ceilings on time and savings deposits.

Mutual savings banks have no legal cash reserve requirements but keep about three percent of their assets as balances with commercial banks to be used for day to day operations. Instead of reserve securities, they try to maintain a ten percent surplus out of earnings in their accounts. Unlike commercial banks, the bulk of their earnings comes from investments in long-term obligations strictly regulated by the banking laws of the states in which they exist. Since 1950, they have been permitted to invest in federally underwritten mortgages and on property outside their own states.

In New York, which serves as a model for other states, limits for certain investments have been set. In general, the tendency has been to restrict investments to real-estate mortgages, to government, railroad and public utility bonds, and occasionally to specific types of corporate stocks and bonds, although twelve states permit the investment of small percentages of deposits at the bank's discretion or make provisions for extending the list of permissible investments upon bank application.

All the states currently allow passbook loans and some personal loans secured by qualified collateral such as life insurance policies. A few have cautiously sanctioned consumer loans if they are based on prudent risk and good security. Almost all banks have been allowed to invest up to five percent of their assets in educational loans.

In the fifty years from their establishment to the Civil War, savings banks grew rapidly in the industrial cities of New England and the Middle States. They were virtually nonexistent elsewhere, and did not follow the expanding frontier westward where other types of financial institutions arose to meet the needs of the developing economy. Although the banks have retained their importance and influence in the Northeast, they have not increased in numbers. From a peak of 666 in 1875 they have declined to slightly less than 500 in 1972. However, in the eighteen states in which they do business under special provisions of the banking laws, they hold more than a third of the total "deposit type" savings of individuals. (See Appendix D, Item 1.) The three leading savings bank states, Massachusetts, Connecticut and New

York, with three-quarters of all mutual savings banks, harbor four-fifths of the deposits.

Obviously, savings banks have gone far beyond their original, philanthropic purposes. They no longer serve only the disadvantaged and low-income groups but are a source of additional income for people at all income levels. At the same time other savings plans have become popular. Primarily because of restrictions imposed by states on their lending and investment programs, the competitive position of savings banks is at a disadvantage today. In ten of the eighteen states in which they exist, they may not open branches. Bound by early traditions, they do not accept deposits from business firms (except pension accounts) or lend money to them and are highly limited in making consumer loans. They may not use certain types of incentives to save such as bonus or notice accounts. State laws also fix maximum balances for individual depositors although they may have as many different savings accounts in as many banks as they please. At present the statutory moratorium on converting to stock companies has been extended two years. Partially as a result of these limitations, savings and loan associations, providing almost identical services as mutual banks, have been outstripping them for many years.

Savings and Loan Associations

Savings and loan associations stem from early nineteenth century building societies designed to help the thousands pouring into industrial regions to house themselves. The first building and loan association in the United States was organized in the small factory town of Frankford, Pennsylvania, to aid the newly arrived workers in the textile and tanning mills to build homes. The Oxford Provident, as it was called, was supervised by thirteen unpaid trustees elected for one year from the members who mutually shared ownership and management. The funds of the society came solely from small, monthly payments for each one's share. When $500 had been accumulated, the trustees granted a loan to erect a house to the one who offered the highest premium. The lucky man made monthly payments with interest. When the fund amassed another $500 the loan procedure was repeated until each member had received his loan. What was left was then divided among the shareholders and the Provident went out of business.

In 1893 when the U.S. Bureau of Labor made its first

nationwide estimate, it found 5,860 building and loan associations in full-time operation throughout the country. Since their inception, the associations, anxious to increase their funds, have added nonborrowing members able to join at any time and professional staffs to direct their activities. They offer three basic types of accounts: a regular savings account with a passbook to record deposits and withdrawals, a bonus account which offers an extra dividend for systematic saving, and an investment account which issues dividend-bearing paid-up savings certificates, usually in $100 or $200 amounts, redeemable at the option of the holder. Savings accounts in these associations are really payments for shares of stock. The depositors are not creditors as in banks but "holders" of an equity receiving dividends rather than interest. Nor is their mutuality destroyed by lending money to nonmembers. (Rummens v. Home Savings and Loan Ass'n. 183 Wash 589.)

Today, although growing extensively in the West, almost two-fifths of the associations are found in four states--Pennsylvania, Illinois, New Jersey, and Ohio. Since 1933, they may be incorporated under national law as well as state law. Almost one-third are federally chartered and supervised by the Federal Home Loan Bank Board, which also may supervise noninsured state members. The Federal Home Loan Board, born in 1932, directs a system of twelve banks operating somewhat like the Federal Reserve. Federal savings and loan associations are required to become members and state-chartered associations and insurance companies may become members or nonmember borrowers. The chief function of the Home Loan banks is to make short-term loans for temporary needs of their members or long-term amortized loans to supplement their members' home financing programs. Shortly after the Home Loan system was inaugurated, the federal government set up the Federal Savings and Loan Insurance Corporation to insure share accounts up to $10,000. Its development has paralleled the FDIC. Federal associations must belong and approved state associations are welcomed.

Savings and loan associations invest most of their funds in loans on real estate. Federal associations are limited to first mortgage loans, originally for not more than $35,000, recently raised to $55,000. In fact, the investment practices of mutual savings banks and building and loan association are very much the same. The popularity of the associations' methods of installment repayment in home financing have made them a major source of help to homeowners throughout the nation.

Because of their low cost of administration and relatively high return on their earning assets, savings and loan associations are able to pay the highest interest of all thrift institutions. However, in time the differences in rate between mutual savings banks and savings and loan associations have disappeared to a large extent, or at least have remained with fairly constant interest payment differentials. The growth of savings and loan associations may be due more to the location of their offices than interest differences. Nevertheless, savings and loan associations are becoming the nation's largest holders of savings deposits. In 1972 the savings capital of the 5,669 associations amounted to $146,322 million. (See Appendix D, Items 3 and 4.)

Competition with Commercial Banks

In recent years competition between commercial banks and thrift institutions has intensified. By the early 1950s commercial banks had begun to rely more and more on time and savings deposits for loanable funds. Thus, a new and powerful competitor capable of offering more and varied services than the thrift institutions entered the struggle for depositors. Furthermore, yield from bond markets became attractive to depositors, especially U.S. Treasury offerings in the sixties. Banks, especially the more limited thrift institutions, began to chafe at government restrictions on their operations. The in-fighting for favorable government rulings became desperate. The Federal Home Loan Board, for instance, is intending to allow federal S and Ls to offer a full range of bill payment and loan service to their shareholders in 1975 instead of only for housing and housing-related items, as at present. Commercial banks anxious to keep present restrictions imposed by their pressure in 1970 view the board's prospective ruling as another attempt to permit checking accounts to pay interest. In turn, thrift banks regard the combination of savings accounts and checking services currently offered by commercial banks as very much the same thing.

The present moratorium on conversions of mutual savings and loan associations and mutual banks to stock companies has been extended to 1976, but some forty test conversions of savings and loan associations have been permitted. However, the attempts of mutual savings banks to secure federal charters--a move prompted by lack of charter legislation for them in two-thirds of the states--has been uniformly rejected by Congress since the thirties. About the only clear-cut solution to the problem of specialized institutions that may have to operate in wider fields to compete effectively is to let all banks try every field. So far such a suggestion has received little support.

Chapter 6

POWERS AND LIMITATIONS OF BANKS

Banks are business institutions whose basic ability to make a profit depends on receiving deposits and extending credit by making loans or discounting notes. In the course of time they have developed various ways of extending their business but, in general, they can only do that which is authorized by specific laws pertaining to them. "The United States statutes relative to national banks," states a federal court decision, "constitute the measure of authority of such corporations and they cannot rightfully exercise any powers except those expressly granted or incidental to carrying on the business for which they were established." (California Nat. Bk. v Kennedy 167 US 362) Moreover, the interpretation and construction of the National Bank Act by the federal Supreme Court are binding upon state courts. (Chemical Nat. Bk. v Havernale 120 Cal 601).

Ultra Vires Acts

Accordingly, persons doing business with a bank must search for its powers and limitations in the statutes under which the bank came into being. If a bank acts beyond the powers either expressedly or impliedly vested in it by law, it commits what is called an ultra vires act. A bank may plead ultra vires as a defense against carrying out the terms of a contract that it has entered. However, it cannot by pleading ultra vires retain money and property obtained by such a contract. A national bank, for instance, that purchases notes which it holds as collateral security when it has been directed to sell them to a third party, may be liable for their value as a conversion, even though it was not within its power to sell them as the owner's agent. (First Nat. Bk. v Anderson 172 US 573).

Real Estate

To prevent banks from speculating in real estate, statutes usually restrict purchase or sale by them. Nevertheless, when such transactions are necessary to protect a bank from losses from loans made by it, they are commonly considered within its power. (Mapes v Scott 88 Ill 352). Property which a bank is not ordinarily empowered to buy may be acquired as security for a loan or as payment for a debt past due. (Steiger v Wood 290 Ill app 48). If a bank engages in a speculative deal for the purchase of real estate, it cannot seek specific performance although a bank's procuring of more real estate than authorized by its charter is not void. (Bank of Michigan v. Miles 1 Dougl. (Mich) 401). It acquires a good title and may enforce a contract of a third person to purchase. (Banks v. Poitiaux 3 Rand (Va) 136).

Unless banned by statute, a state or foreign bank may take mortgages on real estate to secure its loans. A national bank likewise may take a mortgage restricted to seventy-five percent of appraised value for twenty years to secure a debt previously contracted. Federal law allows any national banking association to make real estate loans secured by first liens upon improved real estate, including improved farmland as well as business and residential property. Under provisions of the Housing and Community Development Act of 1974, revising section 24 of the Federal Reserve Act, national banks are allowed to make loans on unimproved real estate and reinvest up to one hundred percent of time and savings deposits in real estate loans. The new law also exempts many loans guaranteed by federal and state governments and agencies from aggregate lending limitations, permits commercial paper discounts on certain short-term construction notes, and extends maturities on certain forest tract loans from three to fifteen years. Where a bank has the power to acquire certain real estate, it may, in most cases, as part of the transaction assume and agree to pay a mortgage on the real estate.

Business Other than Banking

A bank is not a conglomerate. It cannot carry on any business but banking. However, in order to protect itself from loss while pursuing its accustomed business, it may be forced to conduct a totally dissimilar enterprise. (Merchants' State Bk. v Tufts 14 ND 238). For example, a bank that had taken over a warehouse to secure a claim could not defend against a demand for grain stored there by maintaining its charter did not allow it to engage in the business of warehousing. (German Nat. Bk. v Meadowcraft 95 Ill 124). Similarly, a bank may not enter into a partnership with other corporations or individuals, but if it does so by promising a share of the assets to somebody who will run a business it has had to take over, it can't claim all the assets on the ground that the partnership was against the law. (Snow Hill Bk & T Co v D.J. Odorin Drug Co 188 NC 672). Neither state nor national banks have implied power to engage in business by selling or purchasing merchandise even though they may be authorized to buy and sell exchange, bullion, bank notes, government stocks, and other securities. (Jensen v Citizens' Saving Bk 122 NY 135).

Borrowing Money

State and national banks as well as savings banks have the power to borrow money. Where there is a legal restriction on how much a bank may borrow, every person who deals with it is deemed to have notice of the limit. An innocent lender to a bank that has exceeded its prescribed loan limit is not affected by that fact if his own loan is within the limitation. (Am. Southern Nat Bk v Smith 170 Ky 512).

Investments

Although a bank's contract for the purchase of common stock is not necessarily beyond its powers, such investment is illegal as against public policy except when permitted by statute. (Dyer v B'way Central Bk 252 NY 430). This restriction is especially applicable to savings banks in order to protect small depositors. Banking corporations authorized by statute to buy the stock of another corporation may also enter into contracts to buy stocks. (Clucas v Bk of Montclair 110 NJ 394). National banks subject to limitations imposed by the comptroller of currency may purchase investment securities for their own account but may not buy stock in other corporations except as specified by the National Banking Act. They may not procure the stock of a savings bank or another national bank. (Scott v Deweise 181 US 202). While national banks may buy and sell stocks for the accounts of customers, they cannot be held liable for a contract of stock purchase in another corporation for a customer. (Cassat v First Nat Bk 111 NJL 536). However, a national bank may become the owner of shares in another corporation either through payment of a debt owed to the bank or in foreclosure of stock pledged to it as collateral security. (Germania Nat. Bk v Case 99 US 628). In other words, it may acquire such stock in the ordinary course of business and become subject to all the rights and liabilities of similar stockholders. (California Nat Bk v. Kennedy 167 US 362).

A bank may loan money on the security of its own stock, but cases differ as to whether it can in lieu of an authorizing statute purchase its own stock except when necessary to save itself a loss. (Abeles v Cochran 22 Kan 405). Purchases by national banks of their own stock are definitely invalid unless by doing so they save themselves from a loss on a preexisting debt. Nevertheless a subsequent buyer in good faith from the bank gets good title to the stock versus the bank and its creditors. Only the federal government can question the validity of stock purchases or loans on its stock. (Lantrey v Wallace 182 US 536).

For both national and state banks it is ultra vires to agree to repurchase mortgage or other securities sold by them. (Rothschild v Manufacturers' T Co 279 NY 335).

Loan of Credit

Banking corporations, whether state or national, cannot lend their credit to another by acting as security, endorser, or guarantor for him. This is true even if the bank is offered collateral to do so. Such an undertaking is not considered as within the confines of the banking business. (Bridge v Welda State Bk 222 Mo app 586). Nonetheless, the bank may make a guarantee or become a surety or an endorser incidental to its own business or when necessary to protect its own rights. (Eckhart v Heier 38 SD 524). Since a national bank may, for example, discount and negotiate promissory notes, drafts, bills of exchange, and other evidences of debt, such transferring for its own business may be guaranteed. (Peoples' Nat Bk v Manufacturers' Nat Bk 101 US 181). If a bank benefits by a contract of guarantee, it may not reap the fruits of the transaction while repudiating it as ultra vires. So, a national bank helping a builder to complete a structure by guaranteeing payment for needed material is accountable for money handed to it by the builder to pay off a loan. (First Nat Bk v J.L. Mott Iron Works 258 US 240). In the case of negotiable paper the accommodation endorsement of the bank, though ultra vires, renders the bank liable to a good faith holder in due course. (Houghton v First Nat Bk 26 Wis 663).

Fiduciaries

Most banking laws allow banks to act as agents, brokers, or bailees where such a function is incidental to the fulfillment of banking business. Validly, the bank may hold a special deposit, buy securities for a deposit, or, if it is a state bank, lend money for a customer or depositor. The bank is not ordinarily liable for losses if it acts in good faith with due diligence. (Simpson v First Nat Bk 94 Or 147).

It is not within the incidental province of national banks to act as brokers or agents to loan or invest money for depositors or other people even though it may do so for real estate loans. Therefore, a national bank sued for a loss occurring through its negligence in lending a customer's money to an insolvent person without good security may set up its lack of authority to act as a broker in such a transaction. (Grow v Cockrill 63 Ark 118). State banks where there is no statute to the contrary do not face the same prohibition. (Simpson v First Nat Bk 940 RI 147). Since 1962 national banks have been permitted by the comptroller of currency to act as trustee, executor, administrator, registrar of stocks and bonds, guardian of estates of lunatics, or any other fiduciary capacity in which state banks or trusts or other corporations are permitted to act under the laws of the particular state in which the national bank is located.

Transmitting Funds

Banks are authorized by statute to receive and transmit funds, buy and sell exchange, and provide foreign credit for customers. One means of transmitting money or credit is by the purchase of a bank draft, which is a bill of exchange drawn upon a correspondent bank. A bank draft bought and paid for is an executed sale of credit and is not subject to cancellation or revocation. (Int'l. Firearms Co v Kingston T Co 6 NY 2nd 406). The purchaser's remedy for nonpayment is an action for breach of contract. He cannot recover the purchase price of the draft merely because the drawer refuses to stop payment at his request. (Potofsky v Artisans' Savings Bk 37 Del 142). However, where a bank agrees to transmit a specified sum of money to a person abroad, it is an agent of the remitter holding the funds as a trustee until they are actually sent. (Gage v Boston Nat Bk 257 Mass 449). An agreement by a bank to establish credit for a customer is executory to be performed at the place where the credit is to be created. (Richard v American Union Bk 241 NY 163). A remitting bank is duty-bound to act in good faith with reasonable care, skill, and dispatch. (Richard v Credit Suisse 242 NY 346). If the bank has no justifiable excuse for failure to transmit the funds or establish the foreign credit, the depositor is entitled to recover the full sum paid to it. A bank, for example, whose correspondent bank has been unsuccessful in transmitting funds to their destination is liable for the funds even though it has already credited the amount on its books to the correspondent. (Sokoloff v Nat City Bk 250 NY 69).

Bank Notes

By depositing a specified amount of collateral with the proper officials, national banks may have bank notes issued to them which they are empowered to circulate as money. Bank notes or bank bills are the promissory notes of banks to pay the bearer a certain sum of money on demand. Lost bank notes cannot be recovered from the issuing bank, but destroyed or mutilated notes may be replaced if sufficient identification can be made.

Branch Banking

Where branch banking is permitted within a state, the effect is to add another power to the operating certificates of banks. National banks, with the approval of the Comptroller of Currency, may open branches in states in which they are located if state banks are also permitted. A state statute may bar national banks from branching within the state's border. (State ex rel Barret v First Nat Bk 297 Mo 397). Branch banks are considered agents of the parent bank, but in certain situations, such as a process of attachment, the branch may be treated as an independent bank. Ordinarily, a defense valid against either of the two is also valid against the other. (Farmers' Bk v Calk 4 Ky Lr 617). As a principal, the main bank is usually liable for acts of the branch committed by its officers within the scope of their apparent authority. It is also responsible for debts of the branch unless relieved by statute. (Sokoloff v Nat City Bk 221 NY 102). However, a parent bank that cashes a check drawn on a branch before receiving actual notice of a stop payment order is not liable. (Mullinax v American Bk & T Co 189 Tenn 220). Deposits made in a branch are payable only there unless the branch refuses to pay or has been closed or the main bank has a special rule. The insolvency of the principal bank places all branch depositors on the same footing as other creditors of the entire company. (Burleson v Davis (Texas Civ App) 141 SW 559). A foreign branch, even though it acts as an agency of the parent bank, is commonly treated as a separate entity.

Giving Information

Banks are required to give accurate information to depositors about their own accounts. However, they may give information about the financial situation of depositors to others only when the depositor consents or a court order commands. Banks are under no legal obligation to warn the public about the financial condition of their depositors. However a bank giving false information as to the amount standing to the credit of a customer to someone wanting to purchase the latter's business may be liable for damages. (Taylor v Commercial Bank 174 NY 181).

Chapter 7

POWERS OF BANK OFFICERS

Officers and other agents necessary to carry on the business of a bank are usually selected by the directors, or trustees in the case of a savings bank, in accordance with state or federal statutes. By custom or law, such officers are required to furnish bonds guaranteeing their fidelity and insuring the bank against loss through various possible wrongful acts on their part. These bonds are mostly blanket indemnifications against loss through any dishonest or criminal acts and are usually broadly interpreted by the courts. A cashier's bond, for instance, based on "the faithful discharge of the duties of his office" is broken when he violates any valid by-law adopted by the bank (Bank of Carlisle v Hopkins 1 TB Mon (Ky) 245). The investment of large sums of a bank's money in illegitimate transactions by a cashier is covered by the general terms of a bond calling for the faithful and honest discharge of his duties (Wallace v Exchange Bk 126 Ind 265). A cashier's paying of overdrafts made by a depositor of doubtful responsibility is not necessarily criminal, but bank losses thus incurred may be collectible under a fidelity bond (First Nat Bk v Nat Surety Co 243 NY 34).

The bank itself must not fraudulently conceal pertinent material that the surety ought to know before issuing the bond. However, where the bank directors learned that their cashier gambled and required him to increase his bond, the fact that they failed to notify the surety of their cashier's gambling did not discharge the surety from liability for the subsequent defalcations of the cashier (Atlas Bk v Brownell 9 RI 162). A bank must notify the surety of any actual defalcation of an employee but is not required to inform him of mere suspicions (American Surety Co v Pauly 170 US 133). The bank is entitled to recover the whole amount of funds lost through fraud and dishonesty, not merely that which remains after exhausting its remedies (Fitchburg Savings Bk v Mass Bonding & Ins Co 274 Mass 135).

Binding the Bank

Any officer actually engaged in conducting the bank's

business binds the bank. This is also true where he seems to be acting within the scope of his authority whether he is actually endowed with such authority or not (Second Nat Bk v Howe 40 Minn 390). It is the bank's duty to let the public know what an officer is entitled to do. A bank, for example, was held liable for the fraud of an agent employed to solicit business with people of foreign birth when it failed to give notice that he was not authorized to collect funds (Kostoff v Meyer-Kiser Bk 201 Ind 396). While an officer operating within the apparent scope of his authority binds the bank, the person dealing with him is put on inquiry if the act deviates from the ordinary duties of such an officer; for instance, if a cashier makes an agreement with a borrower to sell his collateral at a price far above the market price at the time of the loan, the bank is not bound (Hager v Hagerstown Bk 138 Md 252). Where an officer may benefit personally from a transaction, a customer ought to question whether he is conducting the bank's business or his own (De Baca v Higgins 58 Colo 75). An officer is not acting within the scope of his duties where he promises either to release a debtor from an obligation due the bank or not to enforce liability against him (First Nat Bk. v Tisdale 84 NY 655). Nor can an officer bind the bank by assuring an endorser that he will incur no liability as a result of the endorsement (Cochecho Nat Bk v Haskell 51 NH 116).

Ratification

It is possible for a bank to ratify an unauthorized act of its officer or agent, although it may not necessarily evade responsibility or liability by doing so. If the act was not ultra vires, someone in authority who has the power may either expressly or impliedly ratify it, provided the bank has knowledge of the unauthorized act and the circumstances surrounding it (Citizens' State Bk v Security Bk 54 SD 233). An effective ratification must encompass the entire transaction, assuming its burdens as well as its benefits. For example, a bank that has made a loan on mortgage security through an agent cannot accept the benefits of the agency and enforce the mortgage without being bound by the fraudulent acts and representations of the agent to induce the borrower to enter into the transaction (Kostoff v Meyer-Kiser Bk 201 Ind 396). Where a bank does receive and retain the benefits of an illegal act of an officer it is estopped to deny his authority to make it (Bk of American Nat T & Savings Ass'n v Stotsky 194 Wash 246).

Bank's Liability For Acts of Officers

A bank is liable for the wrongs committed by its officers or agents acting within the apparent scope of their authority (Havens Bk of Tarboro 132 NC 214). If a fraudulent scheme is carried on with the assistance of a cashier, its nature and object being known to him, and his acts are done in the course of his work--receiving money, opening an account, and rushing checks off for quick collection--he represents the bank and renders it, as well as himself, liable (Hobbs v Boatright 195 Mo 693). However, the bank does not become liable for fraudulent acts of its offcers and agents unless the acts concern business that the bank is empowered to do and the representatives are acting within their actual or apparent authority. The misrepresentations of the officer must be the proximate cause of the damage. Where a bank cashier, for instance, gave certain misrepresentations about the credit rating of a customer to an inquirer, the court held that the latter was entitled to rely on the statements and the bank was liable therefor, but there could be no recovery because there was no proof of damage proximately resulting from the misrepresentations (Standard Surety & C Co v Plantville Nat Bk 158 F2d 422).

Where a depositor or other person entrusts property or funds for any valid banking purpose to an officer or agent, the bank is liable if he misappropriates it (Bailey v Union Nat Bk. 159 Tenn 659). A bank whose officer uses the funds of a third person to cover his own overdrafts against the bank is liable to the person defrauded (Nat Bk v Whitney 181 Cal 202). Ordinarily, an officer giving investment advice is considered not to be acting within the scope of his usual business unless long custom without objection by the bank has sanctioned it. However, a bank that gains an advantage due to the advice cannot deny the authority of the officer. Where the bank received no commission or benefit from a sale of stock induced by the false representations of an officer, it may not be chargeable if a loss results (City Nat Bk v Mc Cann 193 Ark 967). Statements of officers as to the quality of bonds are generally considered mere opinion, casting no liability upon the bank or the officers; but an untrue representation of fact, such as whether the bonds are guaranteed by an agency of government, may make the bank liable even if the representation was given in good faith (Bullard v Citizens' Nat Bk 173 Miss 450).

To protect the funds and securities of depositors, share-holders and creditors from the illegal acts of officers and agents of banking corporations, federal and state legislatures have established criminal penalties for those who violate their trust. Generally, federal statutes of this nature now refer not only to national banks, but also to Federal Reserve banks, member banks of the Federal Reserve system and banks insured by the Federal Deposit Insurance Corporation. Federal law, for instance, makes it a crime punishable by fine or imprisonment or both for an officer or employee of any bank whose deposits are insured by the FDIC to stipulate for, receive or consent or agree to receive, any fee, commission, gift, or thing of value from any person, firm, or corporation for procuring or trying to procure from such bank any loan or extension or renewal of a loan or a substitution of security, or the purchase or discount or acceptance of any paper, note, draft, check, or bill of exchange by the bank (18 USC par. 220).

Many states have specific laws dealing with the embezzlement of funds by officers or agents of banking corporations. Some jurisdictions also provide by statute that an officer of a savings bank who willfully misapplies any of the moneys, or resorts to any fictitious or colorable loan, transfer or device to avoid any provision of law applying to such bank shall be guilty of a felony (Fitchburg Sav Bk v Mass Bonding & Ins Co 274 Mass 135). Under federal statute it is a crime for any officer, director, agent, or employee of any Federal Reserve or member bank or any bank insured by the FDIC to embezzle, abstract, or willfully misapply any of the moneys, funds or credits of any such bank. This legislation does not invalidate states from trying officers of state banks on the same charges. An act may be criminal in both jurisdictions (Westfall v United States 274 US 256). However, a bank teller entrusted with the bank's funds during the day who enters the bank at night and takes money from the safe must be tried for larceny (United States v Northway 120 US 237).

To misapply funds is to convert them for one's own use willfully, not merely to commit an act of maladministration (United States v Heinze 218 US 547). An agent appointed by vote of the stockholders to wind up the affairs of an insolvent bank is subject to indictment if he willfully misapplies its funds, (Jewett v United States (Cal) 100 F 832) although he has been held not to be an agent under embezzlement statutes (United States v

Weitzel 246 US 353). If an officer of a bank takes money with the intent to defraud the bank by converting it to his own use, he is an embezzler regardless of whether he derives any benefit from his act (United States v Lee (CC NY) 12 F 816). Even if money is not actually withdrawn, an illegal misapplication can occur, as in the case of a cashier who cashes a check drawn on the bank for his own benefit and applies the proceeds to payment of a note discounted by the bank (Geiger v United States (CA 4 Md) 162 F 884). Neglect of prescribed duties or indifference to the welfare of the bank does not necessarily constitute a criminal misapplication of funds. Directors inducing the bank to declare a dividend, when there are no net profits to pay it, cannot be charged with a criminal offense (United States v Britton 107 US 655). Knowledge or assent of the directors of a bank does not relieve an officer of a bank of liability for misapplying funds. Nor does the fact that he was ordered by his superiors to carry out a transaction, if he knows it was fraudulent (Reiger v United States (Ca8 Mo) 107 F 916).

Discounting a poorly secured note, believing that the borrower would be able to pay it at maturity, is not necessarily a misapplication of funds. But if loans and discounts result in injury to the bank, the question whether they were made in the legitimate exercise of business judgment or for the fraudulent advantage of others must be decided (Evans v United States 153 US 584). The same rule applies if an officer pays an overdraft or cashes a check for someone who has no funds on deposit. Proof of unlawful intent plus injury to the bank negates any claim to discretionary judgment in the ordinary course of a day's business (Coffin v United States 162 US 664).

Provided intent to defraud is shown, any official or employee of any Federal Reserve bank or member bank who certifies a check before the covering amount is deposited or evades in any way the law concerning certification is subject to punishment for a crime (Spurr v United States 174 US 728). In many states an officer who certifies his own or somebody else's check when there are insufficient funds to pay it on deposit is guilty of a fraudulent overdraft (State v Scarlett 91 NJL 200). Implied in the federal statutes is the guilt of anyone for aiding and abetting who willingly contributes to a bank official's unlawful misapplication of bank funds even if he does not benefit personally (Coffin v United States supra).

44

False Entries

By federal statute, whoever makes any false entry in any book of any Federal Reserve bank, member bank, national bank or insured bank with intent to injure or defraud such bank or any supervisor of banks or examiner of them is guilty of a crime punishable by fine or imprisonment or both (18 USC par. 1005). Under some state statutes, making false entries in the accounts books of banks is also punishable as a criminal offense. Criminal intent must be spelled out. Where the president of a national bank placed on its books to his own credit at their face value bonds that were worth little, without the consent of the directors or stockholders, the fact that he gave a guarantee of payment on demand constituted an intent to injure the bank by taking wrongful advantage of the credit, even though he was solvent at the time and intended to make his guarantee good (Agnew v United States 165 US 36).

A false entry is one that the person making it knows to be false at the time he makes it and not one merely made through mistake or negligence (United States v Darby 289 US 224). Where, for instance, an officer of a national bank induces persons to leave money in the bank's vaults to make it appear that the bank has more money on hand than it really has, under an agreement not to use the money, and causes it to be entered as a deposit, he makes a false entry (Peters v United States (CA 9 Wash) 94 F 127). Likewise, entering a transaction as a loan secured by collateral to mask the bank's purchase of the collateral as speculation is a false entry (Morse v United States (CA2) 174 F 539). To convict officers of banks under the statute it is not necessary to show that they made the entries themselves, but only that by some means or other they secured it. For example, a bank teller who, to cover up a shortage in his cash, resorted to the practice of withholding deposit slips to an equivalent amount before reaching the bookkeeping department, so as to cause the individual ledger accounts to understate the depositors' balances, thereby makes a false entry (United States v Giles 300 US 41).

False Reports

False entries in reports or statements of banks designed to injure or defraud the bank, other companies, political bodies, or supervisory agencies, like false book entries, are also punishable criminally (18 USC parag. 1005). This applies not only to the periodical reports required of banks to public officials, but also to reports voluntarily offered by the bank (Harper v United States (CA 8 Indian Terr) 170 F 385). Criminal intent again must be shown. Accordingly, unless a national bank officer knows that there is an irregularity in a report and blindly verifies it without investigation, he cannot be held criminally liable for a report that he believes to be true but is in fact false (Cochran v United States 157 US 286). However, it has been assumed that knowledge of a false entry is indicated by the entry itself, especially where a bank is made to appear in better condition than it actually is (United States v Corbett 215 US 233). Some state statutes require a definite intent to deceive for the offense while others do not do so directly (Foreman v State 124 Neb 74).

To make public officers aware of the condition of a bank, its report is expected to contain a true account of the bank's situation taken from its books. Obviously, a report can be an authentic copy of the books, which may in fact be inaccurate. A whole range of violations may occur from overstating to understating or omitting or concocting facts. The bank's gold reserve, for instance, may be overstated or the amount owing to the bank by an officer may be understated. Frequently, items may be stated under the wrong heading. Overdrafts must not be reported as loans and discounts. An officer who knows they are entered as "cash in hand" on the books makes a false entry when he includes them in the report as cash (United States v Youtsey (CC Ky) 91 F 864). However, when officers properly allow a depositor credit for a larger sum than appears on the credit side of his account and checks are drawn against such credit, an individual who reports these checks as loans and discounts is not guilty of making a false entry (Grave v United States 165 US 323).

Illegal Loans

Since many bank failures have been caused by self-serving loans of bank funds by officers, agents, stockholders, directors and employees of banks, statutes regulating or banning such loans are numerous. Violators are subject to various penalties imposed by the statutes, which are generally strictly construed. Intent to defraud does not have to be shown. However, a renewal of a loan is not considered a loan, but simply a continuation of a debt (State v Love 170 Miss 666). Where a bank officer is a partner in another enterprise, a loan to the partnership may be lawful if the partnership is considered a legal entity and not a cover for making an illegal loan to the bank officer. If the partnership is not considered a legal entity, officers permitting such a loan are criminally liable (People v Knapp 206 NY 373).

Deposits after Insolvency

Most states have enacted laws making it a crime for bank representatives to receive deposits when they are aware that the bank is insolvent. Such statutes apply to savings banks and savings and loan associations as well as trust companies but not to national banks (State v Beach 147 Ind 237). The intent to defraud necessary for criminal liability is sometimes expressly made an essential element in the offense by the statute. But if it is not, it can be construed either as a fraudulent intent to conceal the bank's inability to pay its obligations or to subject a person's money to illegal risk of loss (Griffin v State 142 Ga 636).

It is not necessary under the terms of most of these statutes that the bank be officially declared insolvent if it is in an unsafe condition, known to its officers, and keeps its doors open nevertheless (Banks v State 185 Ark 539). The determination of insolvency is either the inability of the bank to pay its obligations as they become due in the daily conduct of business or the inadequacy of the cash value of its assets, realizable in a reasonable period by prudent persons, to equal its liabilities.

Knowledge of the insolvency by the one accused is usually expressly made a required element in the crime. Opinion is divided as to whether negligence in failing to discover the insolvency is equivalent to knowledge. An Indiana case has held that mere mistake or negligence in failing to acquire knowledge of insolvency did not, as a matter of law, afford sufficient ground upon which to base a conviction of a teller for fraudulent recovery of a deposit (Walter v State 208 Ind 231). However, many courts take the view that it is criminal negligence for one doing a banking business not to know of his own insolvency (Johnson v Larsen 177 Minn 60).

The deposit that is illegally received must be a general one making the bank a debtor, and not a special one only for safekeeping (Snively v State 107 Miss 118). It can be either money or checks as well as a deposit for which a time certificate of deposit is issued (State v Shover 96 Wis 1), although a renewal of a certificate of deposit, where neither money nor interest was added, was ruled not to constitute a deposit since it merely extended the time of payment (Barsness v Tiegen 184 Minn 188).

47

To hold officials liable for receiving deposits while knowing the bank to be insolvent, it is not necessary for them to take the deposits personally. It is sufficient that the directors or managing officers kept an unsafe bank open even if they were not present when the cashier or other employee accepted the deposit (Coblentz v State 164 Md 558). Some statutes specifically provide for the punishment of not only those who receive the deposit but all those who are accessory to or permit or connive at the acceptance of the deposit (State v Easton 113 Iowa 516).

Statutes that concern themselves only with the unlawful receipt of a deposit do not require that loss be shown. But where statutes do make loss to the depositor an indispensable element of the offense, full repayment to him quashes the liability of those accused (Meadowcraft v People 163 Ill 56). The fact that the depositor owes money to the bank does not make the receiving of the deposit any less illegal unless the statute says so. Even under statutes that expressly exclude as unlawful a deposit made by a debtor of the bank, if the indebtedness is not due and payable at the time of the deposit, the receiver can be prosecuted (State v Beach 147 Ind 74). However, a deposit to meet an existing overdraft is not considered a type that makes it a criminal offense for an official of a shaky bank to receive (Ellis v State 138 Wis 513).

Chapter 8

DEPOSITS

A bank's acceptance of a deposit creates a relationship that has undergone substantial legal scrutiny. Although banks seem to be perpetually seeking depositors, not everyone is entitled to become one. A bank may select its customers arbitrarily. Its refusal to accept an account is not open to question (Josell v Riggs Nat Bk 36 App DC 159). It may even return a deposit after receipt and reject any further transactions (Elliot Capital City State Bk 128 Iowa 275). As a rule, the bank and the depositor enter into an implied contract. The depositor presents his deposit, the bank accepts it and assumes the obligation to pay out on his demand a sum equal to the deposit, with or without interest, depending on the nature of the contract. A debtor-creditor relationship is established. The funds belong to the debtor bank as soon as they are deposited (Gibraltar Realty Corp v Mt Vernon T Co 276 NY 353). It may use them as it pleases. If they are lost, destroyed or stolen, the bank is liable for them even if it is free from fault or negligence.

Special Deposits

However, in the type of savings bank in which depositors share proportionally in the profits and losses and in which the managers of the funds are merely trustees and agents of the depositors, the debtor-creditor relationship does not exist (Wells v Black 117 Cal 157). Nevertheless, since the depositor may withdraw his money as the regulations permit, title to the funds in that respect pass to the bank and a debtor-creditor relationship ensues. Where money is left with a bank under an arrangement that the funds are to be turned over to a particular person to pay a particular debt, it does not become the property of the bank (Andrew v Union Savings Bk & T Co 220 Iowa 712). The deposit is a special one. The bank is merely a trustee without any discretion to use the money as its own. The ordinary debtor-creditor relationship is also vitiated where a third person without an expressed or implied contract deposits money to the credit of another. The bank is in the position of holding the property of another without his consent (Re Franklin T Co 30 Pa Dt C 123). A bank gains no title, for example, to a man's money deposited by his wife without authority in a bank where they had no account previously even though the bank had no notice that the wife had neither title to the money nor authority to deposit it (Patek v Patek 166 Mich 446). In the event of insolvency, the depositor is entitled to preference in the distribution of assets if his special deposit has been mingled with the general funds of the bank (Casper v Joyce 54 Wyo 198).

Proof of Deposit Passbooks

Proving that a deposit has been made is not always as simple as it seems. A bank deposit slip is a receipt but it is not conclusive, and oral evidence will be allowed to contradict it (Rosenthal v Citizens' Bk of Cortez 129 Colo 35). So, too, may entries in a passbook be explained or refuted by the depositor or the bank. Although the prevailing view is that rules and regulations printed in a passbook are part of the contract between the bank and the depositor, even though he does not understand English (Larrus v First Nat Bk 122 Cal App2d 884), there are cases that hold that the rules must be called to the attention of the depositor and agreed to by him (Los Angeles Inv Co v Home Savings Bk 180 Cal 601). Mere possession of a savings bank passbook or commercial bank deposit book does not establish the right to make a withdrawal (McCabe v Union Dime Savings Bk. 150 Misc 157 NY 449), nor is a bank under a legal obligation to replace a lost book, although losing it does not preclude recovery of his money by the depositor.

Reporting Discrepancies

A passbook regulation may request the depositor to examine his passbook or checkbook and cancelled checks reporting discrepancies within a certain period of time to the bank. Failure to do so may release a bank from liability for some losses. In a New York case, a bank was held not accountable for the proceeds of checks deposited to the endorser's credit, but converted by his employee to his own account, because the depositor failed to give notice that his checks were not being credited due to the fact that he had delegated the examination of his monthly statement to the guilty employee (Potts & Co v Lafayette Nat Bk 269 NY 181). Even though a husband made a withdrawal from a joint account with his wife, without presenting the required passbook, the withdrawal was held binding on the wife because she failed to object to her husband's withdrawal until about four years after receiving the bank statement showing it (Forbes v First Camden Nat Bk & T Co 25 NJ Super 795). Generally, most cases hold that if a depositor doesn't complain about entries in bankbooks or periodic statements for an unreasonable length of time, both will be considered accounts stated, binding upon bank and depositor, unless duly challenged for fraud or error. Nevertheless, the crediting of interest in a savings bank depositor's passbook does not constitute an account stated (Hoeffler v American Savings Bk 47 NYS2d 327).

A bank deposit may be transferred or assigned. The delivery of the deposits book has been held to be sufficient to constitute a pledge of the book and money on deposit although the bank is customarily entitled to a written notice of a transfer of his account by the depositor (Gibraltar Realty Corp v Mt Vernon T Co 276 NY 353). This does not make a savings bank passbook a negotiable instrument even when the depositor has agreed that the bank may make payments to any person producing it (Ornbaum v First Nat Bk 215 Cal 72).

General and Special Deposits

Although deposits may be classified in many ways, they fall into two distinct groups--general and special deposits. General accounts are those in which the bank gives the depositor credit against which he may draw in the usual course of business. A special deposit is delivered to the bank to be held separate and distinct from the general assets of the bank and to be returned intact upon demand to the depositor who has never renounced title to it. It can consist only of those things deemed part of regular banking business--notes, stocks, bonds, securities, bills of exchange, and even "valuables" of the customers. Money, as we have seen, left for special purpose only, is a special deposit. The bank is not expected to convert itself into a "pawnbroker's shop, cold storage establishment or a warehouse" (Andrew v Union Savings Bk & T Co 220 Iowa 712). The burden of proving that the deposit is special is on the claimant. The distinction between general and special deposit becomes especially important if the bank becomes insolvent.

Bank accounts may be instituted in the name of two or more persons. If depositors own the funds in common, upon the death of one, his estate takes over his interest in the account. The intention of the parties in creating the account determines whether the account belongs only to one of them or is held by both as tenants in common or as joint tenants with the right of survivorship in each (Clift v Grooms (Okla) 331 P2d 382). Ordinarily, where a bank account of two depositors is made payable to either or the survivor, the right of survivorship exists (Re Ivor's Estate 4 Wash 2d 477). An initial agreement between depositors and the bank to provide a joint deposit is generally revocable and can be altered or withdrawn by agreement of the parties (Johnson v Nat Bk 213 SC 458).

To establish a joint account the depositors must be competent (Application of Zenzen 6 176 NYS 2d 853). If one joint depositor becomes incompetent, the predominant view is that his guardian may withdraw an essential maintenance allowance for him, leaving his estate, if he remains incompetent, with a potential right of survivorship (Howard v Imes 265 Ala 298). However, court rulings in different jurisdictions vary widely on the effect of incompetency. In all such cases the obligations and liabilities of the bank depend upon the contract made with the depositor and are unaffected by controversies between the depositors and their representatives (Manta v Kahl 348 Ill App 373).

Bank accounts payable to the order of husband and wife with the balance at the death of either going to the survivor are enforceable after the death of one, warranting the payment of money remaining on deposit to the survivor (First Nat Bk v Lawrence 212 Ala 45). Although competent evidence may show that money on deposit in the name of husband and wife belongs exclusively to one spouse, if nothing intervenes, the money as a rule will be considered as belonging one-half to each (Bowling v Bowling 243 NC 515). Nevertheless, a Wisconsin case has held that a bank account in the joint names of husband and wife becomes legally the property of the wife the moment the husband dies and constitutes no part of the husband's estate regardless of the disposal of the one-half interest in his will (Re Parker's Will 273 Wis 29).

The law of the place where the "and" or "or" deposit was made and kept governs disputes as to ownership and rights pertaining to these accounts, including those of husband and wife

(Kelly v Kelly 134 NJ Eq 316). The courts seem divided on the question of whether or not an owner of an account who feloniously kills his joint tenant can benefit as survivor. An Ohio decision held that such a murder, in the absence of a pertinent statute, did not forfeit the murderer's interest in the joint property (Oleff v Hodapp 129 Ohio St 432), since it emanated from the contract of deposit and not the estate of the deceased owner. But a New York opinion differed sharply on the same set of facts (Bierbraurer v Moran 279 NYS 176).

Sometimes, an individual, for various reasons, deposits his own money for the account of himself and another. Usually he wants to create a genuine joint interest in the other depositor either for the present or after his death. The nature of the account depends on his intention (Austin v Summers 237 SC 613). However, these intentions may not have been made clear before his death. Has the other person a right to the funds as survivor? The courts are divided on what evidence constitutes intention. Some hold that the mere fact that the deposit was made presumes it was a genuine joint account. Where courts do decide the account is joint and survivorship is effective, it is usually on the theory of gift or trust. Where it is clear that the depositor found it difficult to get to a bank and the account was a mere convenience for withdrawals, the other party secures no interest whatever (Re Lewis' Estate 194 Miss 480). A desire to create a joint account is particularly apparent where the deposit is made by a husband or wife in both their names and, if no contrary evidence intervenes, such a presumption is usually made (Menger v Otero County State Bk 44 NM 82).

Deposits In The Name Of or In Trust For Another

When a person deposits his own money to the credit of another or in trust for another he evokes several questions. Obviously, he intends to create a trust but what kind? Is the trust merely tentative or irrevocable? Can the beneficiary enforce it? The intent of a donor of a savings bank trust must sometimes be spelled out by examining the circumstances surrounding the making of the trust. Notification to the beneficiary or other people by the donor of his intention to make such a trust would be substantial evidence of its existence. If the depositor indicates a clear and unqualified purpose to set up an irrevocable trust, he cannot later revoke it by withdrawing his funds. If he does so they will still be considered in trust even if he fails to notify

53

the beneficiary (Minor v Rogers 40 Conn 512). The current rule, called the "Totten Trust" doctrine, states that a deposit of one person of his own money in his own name as trustee for another without any extraneous circumstances does not establish an irrevocable trust during the lifetime of the depositor; he may revoke it at any time he pleases or change it to an irrevocable trust (Re Totten 179 NY 112). If he doesn't so change it, the presumption is that a Totten trust becomes absolute only at the time of the depositor's death. Cases differ widely as to whether the beneficiary must have been informed by the depositor to create an enforceable trust.

A deposit in an individual's name alone may be construed as a trust if the individual who asserts the claim can prove intention on the part of the depositor (Kellen v Snow 185 Mass 288). This is also true of the attempt to prove that a depositor of money to the credit of another intends to make a gift although here the proof that the donee has been informed of the gift and has accepted it is usually needed. Some cases indicate that a depositor's declaration of his intention to make a gift when he opens an account in the name of another makes the gift effective, but others hold that a surrender of the passbook is necessary also (Ruffalo v Savage 252 Wis 175). However, even where a passbook has been delivered to another, a deposit in his name is not inevitably a gift unless there was an intention to make it so (Boyle v Dinsdale 45 Utah 112).

A tentative trust may be revoked at any time and without a formal notice to the beneficiary. Revocation may take place by withdrawal of funds or merely notice of revocation, either orally or in writing. The death of the beneficiary before the donor of the trust terminates it (Re United States T Co 102 NYS 271).

Deposits of Commercial Paper

When checks or other commercial paper are deposited, they are most often treated as cash and the usual debtor-creditor relationship between the bank and the depositor ensues. Sometimes the bank is merely an agent for the owner in collecting funds represented by the commercial paper. Title to paper for such special purpose remains in the depositor. Thus, a different legal situation occurs if the paper is dishonored and not paid. Intention again is the determinant of whether such drafts are to be designated as collection or loan items. Intention must be decided as of the date the deposit was made and not in the light of subsequent events. Where paper is made payable directly to the bank and accepted by it as a deposit there is no doubt that legal title passes to the bank. Otherwise, the rules vary greatly in ferreting out the intentions of the parties (Ditch v Western Nat Bk 79 Md 192).

Special Deposits

Banks receiving special deposits are bound by the general rule of bailments--that so long as a bailee exercises that degree of care and diligence required by law of his class of bailees, he is free of liability even if the thing bailed is lost, destroyed, or stolen. Accordingly, if a bank, without fee, is bailee for the accommodation of the depositor, its liability is limited to gross negligence. If bonds are held by a bank as collateral security, a bailment for the mutual benefit of bailor and bailee exists and the bank is liable only if it does not use ordinary diligence and reasonable care to see that the bonds are not lost, stolen, or destroyed (Gray v Merriam 148 Ill 179). In a case where a bank transmitted negotiable bonds, the court held that ordinary care and diligence required the bank to select a responsible method of transportation, which is not fulfilled by sending such bonds by ordinary mail or registered mail uninsured (Preston v Prather 137 US 604).

Usually, a bank which has not been negligent is not liable for the loss of a special deposit for whose custody it receives no compensation. However, a bank can be liable for retaining in its employ an unfit person. Cases vary widely in assessing unfitness (Merchants' Nat Bk v Guilmartin 88 Ga 797). A Pennsylvania case held that the mere fact that an employee who stole a special deposit had also been stealing the funds of the bank for two years, while making false entries in the books, does not show of itself that the bank was negligent (Scott v Nat Bk. 72 Pa 471). But a Kansas court, pinning liability on a bank whose cashier had absconded with a special deposit, leaving no record of it, proclaimed that the act speaks for itself (Miller v Viola State Bk. 121 Kan 93). A bank must determine the right of anyone to whom it delivers property to receive it. Therefore, though it acted in good faith in delivering to a husband property deposited and belonging to his wife, it was liable for the wrong delivery (Kierce v Farmers' Bk 174 Ky 22).

Certificates of Deposit

When in the late 1950s large investors began to shift their cash lying idle in demand deposits to interest-bearing Treasury bills and similar securities, banks were forced to find some way to "buy" money to meet strong credit demands. A new kind of time deposit earning interest, called a negotiable certificate of deposit, was the answer. A CD could be purchased from a bank by depositing a sum of money for a fixed period of time. If the purchaser needed money before the CD became due, he sold it. CDs are a standard source of money for banks today.

Since a certificate of deposit is an acknowledgment by a bank of the receipt of money with an engagement to repay, it creates a debtor-creditor relationship between the depositor of the money and the bank. Dependent on the time of payment, CDs are classified as either time or demand certificates. Basically, the rules applicable to other types of deposits apply to them. A certificate of deposit has the characteristics of a promissory note and to all intents and purposes operates exactly like one (Uniform Commercial Code Parag. 3-104 (1) (2) c). However, under certain circumstances the certificate may not be negotiable; for example, if it does not comply with statutory requirements or is payable only to the depositor himself (International Bk v German Bk 3 Mo App 362).

Payment and Recovery

A bank which issues a negotiable CD pays the amount on the face of the certificate to the holder irrespective of whether or not it is the same amount deposited by the depositor (Payne v Clark 19 Mo 152). Parties other than the issuing bank may become liable for payment as co-makers, sureties or guarantors provided there has been some legal consideration for their signing (Looney v Belcher 169 Va 160). Only an authorized officer of a bank may issue one. A CD made out by the cashier of the bank to himself is void on its face and transfers no rights to a purchaser (Lee v Smith 84 Mo 304). Only those authorized by the certificate may receive payment unless the bank has notice that such a person has no real title as, for instance, where the bank knew that the certificate had been endorsed to the holder for the illegal consideration of a gambling debt (Drinkall v Movius State Bk. 11 ND 10).

Rulings differ as to whether or not a demand for payment

must be made before suit can be brought on a CD even though it is regarded as a negotiable instrument on which no demand is necessary (Pierce v State Nat Bk 215 Mass 18). Generally, the certificate must be returned properly endorsed for payment except where it can be shown it was lost or destroyed. In such case, indemnity against future claims may be requested before payment (Kirkwood v First Nat Bk 40 Neb 484). A forged endorsement of the payee's signature does not relieve the bank from payment to the payee if it cashes the certificate for the forger. In a Missouri case where a person stole a certificate, forged the payee's signature thereon and cashed it at a bank which, in turn, received a payment from the issuing bank, both banks were held liable to the payee for conversion (Stout v Benoist 39 Mo 377).

A CD continues to bear interest after its maturity unless it contains a contrary stipulation. Even so, if the bank fails or wrongly refuses to pay at maturity, interest will continue (Citizens' Nat Bk v Brown 45 Ohio St 39).

Safe Deposit Boxes

The right of a bank to rent safe deposit boxes is recognized as a legitimate banking transaction although it is different from taking a special deposit for safekeeping in which the bank does not assume direct control over the deposit (Cussin v Southern Cal Savings Bk 133 Cal 534). When a safe-deposit company leases a box the relationship is a bailor-bailee one (National Safe Dep Co v Stead 250 Ill 584). Such a bailment is terminable at the will or death of the depositor and the deposit company is obliged to return the contents of the box in accordance with the contract and the law. A bank renting boxes must exercise at least ordinary diligence to prevent access to the box of unauthorized persons and to investigate the right of third persons to access even if they possess a key to the box. The bank is not liable for violation of the contract if it admits without special authorization a legally designated deputy who misappropriates the contents of the box (Jones v Morgan 90 NY 4). Whenever third parties, under a color of legal process, demand access to the contents of the box, the bank's duty is to verify if the process warrants the surrender of the property and act prudently if convinced it doesn't (West v State St Exchange 250 Mass 537). In a New York case, in which police officers having a search warrant for stolen goods took away the contents of a box, the bank was held not to have discharged its duty by merely making a formal protest without examining the warrant and checking the contents of the box against it (Roberts v Stuyvesant Safe Dep Co 123 NY 57). If property of a third person is put into the box for safekeeping without informing the lessor, he is not responsible for loss of such property. Where, for example, securities belonging to a daughter of the lessee were stolen from a safe deposit box, the bank was not held liable since it was not informed by the lessee that he was using it for the safekeeping of securities other than his own (Coons v First Nat Bk 218 NYS 189). Boxes may be rented to two or more persons and a right of survivorship created. However, it is necessary to distinguish between a joint use of the box and the survivor's right to the contents. Where a contract is specific on this point or circumstances strongly suggest it, the right of survivorship in the contents will be upheld (Kleeman v Sheridan 75 Ariz 311).

Chapter 9

WITHDRAWALS

A bank is under an implied contract to repay funds from a general deposit, upon proper demand, to a depositor or person designated by him (Eads v Commercial Nat. Bk 33 Ariz 499). No money can be withdrawn from the account, however, without the depositor's signature or those indicated on the signature card (Henderson v Greeley Nat Bk 111 Colo 365). If the depositor has not been negligent or at fault, payments by the bank against checks in which his signature has been forged or amounts altered or unauthorized endorsements made cannot be charged against his account (First Nat Bk v Morgan 58 NM 730). Nor has the bank any implied authority, in the absence of statute, to pay notes of a depositor owing to a third person and charge such payments against his general deposit account (Grissom v Commercial Nat Bk 87 Tenn 350). Usually, the bank makes its payments to the depositor by check or in the case of a savings account by presentation of a passbook. In either method it must exercise ordinary care that the person receiving the payment is entitled to it even where it has a regulation that the mere possession of a passbook is enough to authorize payment. Where the bank paid out money upon presentation of a passbook and a duly authenticated power of attorney, both of which were later shown to have been secured from the depositor by fraud and duress, the bank was not held liable since the production of the passbook and power of attorney was held to be due care (Romero v Sjoberg 5 NY2d 518).

In the absence of statutory authorization, if a joint account is not payable to either or the survivor of the depositors, banks may render themselves liable if they allow withdrawals without the authority of all the depositors (Liner v Commercial Nat Bk 85 Ga App 278). Ordinarily, if each party has a substantial interest in the account, the bank is well advised not to let more than half be withdrawn by one of the depositors without a specific directive.

A bank may pay out a deposit made in the name of a third party if no adverse claim is made by the actual depositor. However, it does so at its own peril. If there is a dispute as to who is entitled to the funds a bank will usually pay to no one until it is legally compelled to do so (Murphy v Nem 51 Mont 82). It has a right to recover money paid out by mistake, even though it has been negligent, provided the recipient has not been damaged (Manufacturers' T Co v Diamond 186 NYS2d 917).

A bank is authorized to pay out deposits of funds in trust strictly in accordance with the contract of deposit. It cannot pay funds to the beneficiary although some statutes allow such payment after the death of the trustee. The bank must assure itself of the legal authority of the trustee. In the absence of information to the contrary, the bank is bound to assume that the fiduciary will use withdrawn funds properly and incurs no liability if he does not. The law imposes no duty on the bank to administer the trust, but if it has notice or knowledge that a trustee is misappropriating or intends to do so, the bank may find itself helping in the commission of a fraud and may be liable if it takes no action (Bischoff v Yorkville Bk 218 NY 106). For example, where the trustee of a decedent's estate drew a check on the estate account to his own order and deposited the check in his personal, overdrawn account in the same bank, thereby paying his own debt to the bank, a Pennsylvania court held that the bank was liable to the beneficiary of the trust for such misappropriation of trust funds (Pennsylvania Co for Ins. on Lives v Ninth Bk & T Co 306 Pa 148).

Withdrawals from Savings Banks

Although it has the right to require notice before a depositor can make a withdrawal, a savings bank cannot postpone or delay payments to him indefinitely if he makes a demand in proper form. A depositor customarily takes out his money himself, but where circumstances, such as illness, prevent, he may send an order correctly witnessed plus his passbook for a withdrawal by another person. The bank cannot avoid liability for payment on a forged order to one who fraudulently secured the passbook even by showing the payment was made in good faith and with due care (Smith v Bklyn Savings Bk 101 NY 58). A savings bank is obligated to use vigilance in paying over a depositor's money so that he may be protected against fraud, larceny, and forgery. Often negligence on a bank's part is due to failure to detect manifest discrepancies in signatures. Even if the depositor is negligent he may collect by an action on contract--the bank agreed to repay his deposits--although there is a New York case in which the depositor, not having notified the bank of the loss of his passbook, could not recover after the bank paid his deposit to an impostor who presented the book (Kelly v Emigrant Savings Bk (NY) 2 Daly 227). As a rule, a savings bank passbook must be presented to draw money. But where an administrator of a deceased savings bank depositor was unable to produce the book, because the family of the decedent wrongly withheld or destroyed it, a Rhode Island court decided that the deposit could be recovered without the passbook (Palmer v Providence Inst. for Savings 14 RI 68). Where it has become impossible for the depositor or his representative to produce the book, recovery of the proceeds is still possible, although the bank may require an indemnifying bond (Miller v First Granite City Nat Bk 349 Ill App 347). No matter how reasonable bank by-laws relating to withdrawal are, ambiguities in them must be resolved against the bank (Commerso v Nat City Bk 21 NYS 2d 187). Usually if the depositor accepts or retains the book, he is deemed to have acquiesced in the rules printed therein.

Attachment and Garnishment

Creditors sometimes try to collect debts owing to them by seeking court orders either to seize the debtor's property (attachment) or to direct third parties to pay them out of funds or credits they hold belonging to the debtor (garnishment). The right to reach deposits by such writs is generally recognized. As soon as funds are deposited in a bank they are subject to such process (Savings Bk v Loewe 242 US 357), whether they are in a general or special account (Lutz v Williams 79 W Va 609). When either writ is served on a bank, the bank may not apply any deposit funds to any debt due from the depositor (Marx v Parker 9 Wash 437). A check drawn on the funds will not take precedence over a subsequent garnishment, provided the check has not previously been accepted or certified (Merchants' & Manufacturers' Nat Bk v Barnes 18 Mont 335).

The garnishing creditor is in the same position as the depositor. If the depositor holds the funds in trust or they belong to another, they cannot be garnished (Home Land & Loan Co v Routh 123 Ark 360). However, the depositor will be considered the owner unless he can prove the contrary. Funds actually belonging to him, but deposited in the name of a third person, may be reached by creditors in a garnishment. Accordingly, money received by a lottery company and deposited by its agent to his credit for the purpose of applying it to the certificate holders of the company remains the money of the company subject to garnishment by anyone holding a claim against it (Fidelity Funding Co v Vaughan 18 Okla 13).

Whether a joint bank account can be attached or garnished at the instance of a creditor of one of the depositors depends on the respective prior rights to the money before depositing and the effect of the agreement between the depositors and the bank when the account was opened. If the agreement makes the interest of each depositor uncertain or contrary no writ can be granted (Fairfax v Savings Bk 175 Md 136). A number of cases simply hold that a joint bank account is a contract between depositors whereby each one gives the other the right to withdraw any or all of the funds deposited so that a creditor of one may attach or garnish without regard to the question of actual ownership (Park Enterprises v Trach 233 Minn 467). Howver, courts are generally more influenced by the title of the depositors than the provisions of the deposit agreement. For example, a joint account in the name of husband and wife was ruled not reachable by a judgment creditor of the husband where the wife was proved the sole owner of the funds of the account (Union Properties Inc v Cleveland T Co 152 Ohio St 430). In some cases, courts have held each depositor to have an equal right to the funds in joint accounts and that a garnishing creditor may recover only half of the money in the account (Catlow v Whipple (RI) 83 A 753).

Prior to a garnishment or after its service, a bank may set off against the amount of the deposit that has been garnished the amount of any matured indebtedness owed to it by the depositor (Holloway v First Nat Bk 45 Idaho 746). Rulings differ as to indebtedness not yet matured and the bank may waive its right of set-off against a garnishing creditor if it wishes (Walt v Bk of America Nat T & Savings Ass'n 9 Cal 2d 46).

Actions to Recover Deposits

Depositors can usually get their money back from a bank by properly demanding it. A demand must be made to maintain an action for deposits except where obviously it would be useless, as in the event that the bank has already denied any liability for sums due the depositor (Leather Manufacturers' Bk v Merchants' Nat Bk 128 US 26). A bank need not pay a deposit on an oral demand or order. A proper demand is made during business hours by presenting a check, order, draft, or other writing for payment, nor need it be for the entire balance in the account

(Lourie v Chase Nat Bk (sup) NYS 2d 205). A bank has a right to close out an account if it deems the customer an undesirable one, but it has the burden of proving it has paid if it offers that defense in an action to recover the account. Generally it is the demand and refusal to pay that sets the Statute of Limitations running. If a long enough time elapses before a demand, a presumption of payment may occur which can only be overcome by very convincing proof to the contrary especially if no claim has been made for twenty years (Boscowitz v Chase Nat Bk 111 NYS 2d 147).

Interest on Deposits

The obligation of a bank to pay interest is a matter of agreement with the depositor. However, banks may not credit interest for regular commercial accounts and usually special deposits. If, however, a demand for a deposit is made and the bank defaults, interest for the defaulted amount starts to run. A savings bank cannot pay interest beyond the limits set by statute. The insolvency of a bank makes its deposits due and interest starts also to run from the day the bank suspends business (American T & Bkg Co v Boone 102 Ga 202). Of course, the insolvency renders the bank's capacity to pay highly doubtful. If a check is paid upon a forged endorsement and the amount wrongfully charged to the depositor, he can draw interest from the date of the charging even if his deposit could not draw interest previously (German Savings Bk v Citizens' Nat Bk 101 Iowa 530).

Liability for Loss

Since the relation between a bank and a general depositor is that of debtor-creditor, the bank bears the cost resulting from theft, destruction or loss of deposits, regardless of its own negligence or fault (Bischoff v Yorkville Bk 218 NY 106). This is also true of commercial paper properly endorsed and deposited in the usual course of business except upon the depositor's liability as an endorser. Likewise, loss in the mail of commercial paper forwarded by a bank for collection after crediting it as money to the account of the depositor falls on the bank (Heinrich v First Nat Bk 21 NY 1). Nor is a bank relieved from liability for loss of a deposit made after banking hours when the bank customarily takes deposits at that time for the accommodation of customers (Farmers' Bk & T Co v Boshears 148 Ark 589).

63

Unclaimed Accounts

A bank has no right in custom or law to retain bank deposits that are not claimed by their depositors. A state may compel the surrender of dormant accounts where there are substantial grounds to believe that they have been abandoned or forgotten, especially if the lawful demands of depositors are not foreclosed. Statutes requiring the turning over to states of deposits unclaimed for a specific period of years have been declared constitutional whether the state merely takes custody or title (Security Savings Bk v California 263 US 282). The limiting of such statutes to only certain kinds of banking institutions is not considered class legislation (Germantown T Co v Powell 265 Pa 711). Statutes requiring the reporting of all unclaimed deposits to the state and providing for the disposal of deposit funds of solvent or liquidating banks may be applied to national banks (Roth v Delano 338 US 226).

Chapter 10

CHECKS

The Uniform Negotiable Instruments Act defines a check as a bill of exchange drawn on a bank and payable on demand. A depository bank is required to pay the check exactly as directed by the depositor (Calloway v Hamilton Nat Bk 900 App DC 420). It must pay only to the payee named on the check or to his order as well as confirm the check's signature with that on the signature card filed with the bank. In the absence of statutory direction, the bank must verify any discrepancy in the amounts expressed by figures and words on the face of the check before cashing it (Kanowitz v Manufacturers' T Co 13 NYS 2d 211). Payment of a check is made by the drawee bank either furnishing money to the payee or endorser, crediting it to his account or issuing a cashier's check to him in return. A cashier's check, which cannot be countermanded except under special circumstances, is a bill of exchange drawn by the bank upon itself. Other types of checks issued by banks are a banker's draft, which is a check drawn by one bank upon another, and traveler's checks, used to make money available to people while traveling. These usually require a purchaser's signature on their face when bought and its repetition when cashed. The second signature is considered a payee's endorsement and gives the check final currency (Sullivan v Knauth 220 NY 216).

Checks may be drawn or endorsed for a principal by a duly authorized agent. Clearly, a bank incurs no liability to a principal when it cashes a check by one who endorses it as an agent, but a Texas case has even held that a payee of checks had no direct cause of action against a bank that cashed checks for the payee's agent without knowing that he lacked authority to endorse them (Strickland Transportation Co v First State Bk 147 Tex 193). If the bank knowingly permits an agent to exceed his authority, it is liable for the money withdrawn. Where a deposit is made in the name of two or more persons, a bank may cash checks in the name of any of the depositors if such a stipulation has been made. However, in the absence of an agreement, withdrawals from joint deposits require the authority of all the depositors and a bank pays a check signed by only one of them at its own risk

(Gish Bag Co v Leachman 163 Ky 720). Nor will the drawing of a check by a joint tenant upon the joint account be honored if presented after his death (Straut v Hollinger 139 NJ Eq 206).

Generally, a check must be presented for payment within a reasonable time after it is issued. A bank will usually ask the drawer whether he still wants a "stale" check cashed. However, unless the Statute of Limitations operates, mere delay should not prevent the payment of a certified check by a drawee bank (Merchants' Nat Bk v State Nat Bk (US) 10 Wall 604). A postdated check is valid, but payment by a drawee bank before its date may open the bank to liability unless the depositor's own negligence or fraud or a previous agreement by the bank intervenes (Kalish v Manufacturers' T Co v Leff 253 NY 359).

Since any condition on the face of the check makes it nonnegotiable, it is the bank's duty before payment to ascertain whether such a condition has been performed to prevent possible liability (Irving Trust Co v Leff 253 NY 359). A bank cashing a check without the payee's endorsement must show payment to the proper person before it can charge the account of the drawer of the check (Soma v Handrulia 277 NY 223). As a rule, a bank is protected in paying checks drawn by an insane person if it has no notice of the insanity, but a few jurisdictions oppose this view (American T Bkg Co v Boone 102 Ga 202).

Drawing a check to the order of a bank prevents using its proceeds for anyone else but the drawer. Consequently when a dishonest employee deposited his employer's checks to his own credit in the bank to which they were made payable, assuring the bank that the checks were in payment of his salary, the bank was held liable to his employer (Fidelity & Casualty Co v Hellenic Bk & T Co 25 NYS 2d 43). Without contravening statutes, a holder of a check loses his right to payment and a bank's authority to pay is revoked if the drawer of a check dies, unless the check has previously been accepted or certified. Nevertheless the bank is protected if it pays without knowledge of the drawer's death (Glennan v Rochester T & Safe Dep Co 209 NY 12).

Although under the Uniform Negotiable Instruments Act, a check does not, of itself, operate as an assignment of any part of the funds credited to the drawer, a bank must honor checks drawn upon it if the depositor has sufficient funds on deposit when it is presented. For failure to do so, the depositor has an action against the bank for damages that he may have sustained because of the bank's refusal (Armstrong v American Exchange Bk 133 US 433). The holder or payee of a check that has been dishonored has a right of action on this account only against the drawer or endorser of the check. The bank is not obliged to make part payment to the extent of funds the drawer has on deposit of a check that is overdrawn.

Certification of Checks

The certification of a check by the bank on which it is drawn is a common necessity of business. Certification changes a check into instant money and a reliable mainspring of credit. The certification of a check transfers the funds represented thereby from the credit of the maker to that of the payee. To all intents and purposes, the latter becomes a depositor of the drawee bank to the amount of the check with the rights and duties of one in such position (Mark v Anchor Savings Bk 252 Pa 304). Unless otherwise agreed, the bank is under no obligation to certify a check. The cashier or teller in most banks is the proper officer to certify. It is a federal crime for an officer, agent, director or employee of a Federal Reserve Bank or member bank to resort to any device to evade the law as to certification of checks. The usual practice of certification is to stamp or write on the check the word "certified" or an equivalent expression with the signature of the certifying officer (First Nat Bk v Whitman 94 US 343). A bank's promise to pay any checks drawn upon it by a named person is a guarantee and not a certification.

When a check is certified, it represents its face value as a deposit payable on demand to the holder. The certification constitutes an admission of the genuineness of the drawer's signature and the sufficiency of funds set aside by the drawee for payment when the check is presented. It does not, however, warrant the genuineness of the body of the check or the payee's signature or the lawfulness of purpose of the check. It cannot be used to show that the holder is a holder in due course (National City Bk v Waggoner 243 NYS 299). The bank has an absolute liability to the holder of the check until discharged by payment or released through the Statute of Limitations. If through error or fraud the bank is induced to certify a check for an amount exceeding the drawer's deposit, it can cancel the certification or countermand payment unless the right of an innocent holder for value has intervened (State v Scarlett 91 NJL 200). Even though the drawer's signature turns out to be forged, a bank is liable to a certified holder because certification has guaranteed the genuineness of the signature.

Since the certification of a check is not a warranty of the amount of the check, if a check has been raised illegally before certification, the prevailing view is that a certifying bank ought not be responsible for the amount of the raised check if it has acted with due care (Clews v Bk of NY Nat Bk Assn 89 NY 418). A bank is also relieved of liability for an alteration after certification done without knowledge, consent or negligence on its part. A forged certification on a check later cashed by the purported certifying bank, binds the bank as if the certification were genuine since the bank should have repudiated it.

Certification of a check at the request of the drawer operates as an assurance that the check is genuine and the certifying bank becomes bound along with the drawer (McIntire v Raskin 173 Ga 746). If the payee or holder of a check has it certified by the drawee bank instead of cashing it, the drawer and the endorsees are discharged. So if a bank fails immediately after a payee has had a check certified by it, the payee has no right of action against the drawer but must look to the bank for payment (Wachtell v Rosen 249 NY 386). Although a bank has the right to refuse certification, this does not mean that the check is dishonored and that the holder has a right to sue the drawer (Robb v Pennsylvania Co 186 Pa 456).

Chapter 11

FORGERY, ALTERATION, AND FRAUD

Forged Signature

Since a bank is bound to know the signatures of its depositors, payment of a forged check cannot be charged against the depositor if he is entirely relieved of fault or negligence. The bank is presumed to be paying the check out of its own funds (Central Nat Bk v First Merchants' Nat Bk & T Co 171 Va 289). The fact that the depositor did not inform the bank of the loss of blank checks or that he has a rubber stamp of his own signature does not constitute negligence on his part. If a forger obtained possession of the stamp through the depositor's negligence, the responsibility for the loss caused by the resulting forgeries would not rest upon the bank, if its cashier exercised due care in inspecting the checks when presented for payment (Redington v Woods 45 Cal 406). As between itself and the drawer, a drawee bank undertakes not to pay checks unless they contain the genuine signature of the drawer, but it cannot recover money paid out to an innocent holder in due course (First Nat Bk v State Bk 107 Iowa 327). Of course, recovery by the bank can be made against forgers or thieves or those who have no title to the check. It can also be made against the holder if he was negligent in taking the instrument, if circumstances were such that a reasonable man would demand an inquiry when he took the check.

A bank that cashes a check drawn upon another bank, without requiring proof of the identity of the person presenting it, cannot hold the proceeds against the drawee bank when the check later proves to be forged. The bank should have required the stranger to identify himself (Farmers' Nat Bk v Farmers' T & Bk 159 Ky 141).

Forged Endorsement

A bank is expected to determine whether the person presenting a check to it for payment is really the payee named in the check. If the endorsement is forged, the bank may find itself out its own funds rather than the drawer's. The fact that the last endorsement

69

on a check is genuine does not relieve the bank of the necessity to examine the authenticity of the previous ones. This doctrine goes so far that in a case where a check payable to a person fell accidentally into the hands of another with the identical name who endorsed and cashed it, the bank was still liable for the amount to the drawer (Fulton Nat Bk v United States 197 F2d 763). If the bank can show it was free of negligence, but the drawer's own negligence was the proximate cause of the loss resulting from the forgery, he may be precluded from collecting. However the negligence must have directly caused the situation. Mailing a check to the wrong person, in itself, or failing to realize the dishonesty of an employee or to notify the bank of his former forgeries have not been considered direct enough to shift the burden from the bank. It has to be an affirmative act like writing the payee's name in pencil very lightly, for instance (U.S. Cold Storage Co v Central Mfg Dist Bk 343 Ill 503).

The depositor has a positive duty to report to the bank any forgeries that he may discover as well as return any cancelled checks paid on forged endorsements when the bank requests them (Showers v Merchants' Nat Bk 293 Pa 241). A depositor owes no duty to a bank to employ none but honest clerks who will not steal money by forging the names of payees on checks stolen from him. If an employee or agent forges the endorsement of his employer or principal, any payments he receives thereby are unauthorized and cannot be charged to the employer or principal. The loss falls on the drawee bank, provided again that the drawer's negligence was not the proximate cause of the forgery. A Washington case held that where an employer over a long period of time gave blank checks to his employee who made them payable to fictitious employees, and, after forging their endorsements, cashed the checks, the employer was negligent, since he failed to check up on people actually in his employ or maintain an adequate system of accounting by which such loss could have been avoided (Defiance Lumber Co v Merchants' Nat Bk 293 Pa 241).

Cases differ sharply under what circumstances a bank paying a check upon a forged or unauthorized endorsement becomes liable to the true payee, although most jurisdictions will sustain a suit by the payee provided his negligence has not been the proximate cause of the forgery. Endorsing a check is an implied warranty of the genuineness of previous endorsements (First Nat Bk v Marshalltown State Bk 107 Iowa 327). Therefore a bank that suffers a loss by paying an endorser whose title to the check is based on a previous forged endorsement may demand

and recover the payment from the endorser, provided the bank itself has not been negligent. Where, for instance, the bank failed to observe the order of the drawer of the check to stop payment, it could not recover (National Bk v First Nat Bk 51 Okla 787).

Altered Checks

In cases where the body of the check is altered, no presumption exists that the drawee bank must know any handwriting except the signature of the drawer. Even so, unless there is definite negligence on the part of the depositor, the drawee bank pays such a check at its peril and cannot charge the payment against the depositor. In an Oklahoma case where the alteration of the check was palpable and apparent by ordinary inspection, the court held the bank liable for paying it even though the drawer had executed it unskillfully in the first place (First Nat Bk v Ketchum 68 Okla 104). However, in general the drawer must be free of contributing to the forgery. Many cases repeatedly rule that careless execution of checks at the time they were signed by a depositor, so as to invite or present opportunity for alteration, affects his right to recover in the event of an unauthorized alteration (Leather Manufacturers' Nat Bk v Morgan 117 US 91). For example, a California case declares that where a depositor signed a blank check and delivered it to his agent who thereafter filled in the blanks fraudulently, the depositor cannot collect for payments made by the bank since it was the depositor's conduct that led the bank to pay the instrument (Wright v. Bk of America Nat T & Savings Assn 176 Cal App2d 176). Nevertheless, the negligence of the depositor in drawing a check may not render him liable where the bank fails to exercise due care in paying a check that has been altered. In a case where the drawer perforated the amount of the check in such a way that further figures could be added, the bank was not absolved from liability for paying the raised amount because the alteration involved not only the change in amount but the obliteration of the name of the original payee and the substitution of the word "cash" (Critten v Chemical Nat Bk 171 NY 219).

Impostors

When a man deceived by an impostor gives him a check which the latter endorses and cashes, the bank is not liable, since the loss is due to the drawer's own error (Emporia Nat Bk v

Shotwell 35 Kan 360). This is true even where the fraud was perpetrated through the mails and the drawer did not actually meet the impostor. The United States government cannot recover from banks that cash refund checks on the endorsements of impostors who fraudulently claim false overpayments on income tax (United States v Bk of America Nat T & Savings Assn 274 F2d 366). However, if the impostor who endorses the check represents himself to be the agent of the payee and not the payee himself, the loss may fall upon the bank (Weaver v First Nat Bk 138 Colo 83). Where, however, a drawer makes a check payable to a nonexistent person, he cannot recover from the drawee bank for paying it on an endorsement purporting to be that of such a person. Where the fact that the person did not exist is unknown to the drawer, the bank is put upon inquiry and if it fails to identify him it should refuse payment (Hayes v Lowndes Savings Bk & T Co 118 W Va 360). Where the negligence of the drawer is the proximate cause of loss, it should fall upon him. For instance, in a situation where a trustee issued checks to a beneficiary for two years after the beneficiary's death, which were cashed by his widow purporting to be her husband's agent, the bank was absolved from liability on the ground of the trustee's negligence (Darling Stores Inc. v Fidelity-Bks T Co 178 Tenn 165).

Stopping Payment

Since a check is only an order upon a bank to pay out money from a depositor's account, it can be revoked or cancelled by the drawer any time before it has been certified, accepted or paid by the bank. If the bank receives a notice from the drawer to stop payment, it must do so. However, the drawer may also withdraw or revoke his order. If the bank has followed orders properly, whatever consequences that ensue must fall upon the drawer. The payee of the check cannot stop payment or require the drawer to stop payment on a check he has already endorsed to the order of another.

After a check has been certified at the request of the drawer, his stop payment order is valid against the payee or an endorsee holder not a holder in due course. However, if the check has been negotiated to a holder in due course, the order has no effect (Potofsky v Artisans' Savings Bk (Sup) 37 Del 151). If a payee or holder of the check secures the certification, it is too late for the drawer to have payment stopped even if he discovers the payee is insolvent (Sutter v Security T Co 96 NJ Eq 644).

A cashier's check is ordinarily beyond the power of the purchaser or the issuing bank to stop payment thereon. In the hands of a holder in due course, it is a primary obligation of the bank and must be honored (Kohler v First Nat Bk 157 Wash 417). The same is true of a bank money order.

To be effective, a stop payment order must be positive and unqualified and must describe the drawer and the check with reasonable accuracy as well as give the name of the payee. The notification to the bank must be clear and consummated, but can be oral unless banned by statute. A notice to a branch bank to stop payment will, as pointed out previously, not make the parent bank liable for cashing the check if it has not had sufficient time to receive the order. Nor, in the absence of statute, can a stop payment notice of one joint owner of a bank account stop payment on a check drawn by the other where each is allowed to draw checks on the account (Ealing v City Nat Bk & T Co 278 Mich 571).

If a bank pays a check after receiving timely notice from the drawer to stop payment, it is liable to him for the proceeds, although it has been held that a bank exercising good faith and reasonable care after receiving a stop payment notice has a valid defense in an action to recover the amount of the check (Speroff v First-Central T Co 149 Ohio St 415).

A depositor may ratify the bank's unauthorized payment of a stopped check by various acts, such as recognizing the payee's receipt of the money as payment of his debt to the payee. Such ratification precludes recovery from the bank. It is a general rule that a depositor cannot make a profit out of a bank's mistake in paying a stopped check but only recoup what is lost (American Defense Soc v Sherman Nat Bk 225 NY 506).

Chapter 12

LOANS AND INTEREST

"Neither a borrower nor a lender be" was never advice offered by a banker. Lending money is the most profitable activity of commercial banks. Deposits furnish a reservoir of funds that banks are only too ready to lend to good credit risks who promise to return the loan with interest and even pledge collateral as security. In applying for such a loan a borrower usually fills out a statement of his financial condition. Any materially false assertion, whether made knowingly or unknowingly, is ground for rescinding the loan (Monier v Guarantee T Co 298 US 670).

To protect the general public numerous statutes, both state and national, have been enacted regulating loans by banks and other financial institutions. The National Bank Act as well as many state laws restrict the amounts that may be loaned to one person so that a bank director of a national bank and others who knowingly assent to an excessive loan are personally liable for any damages the bank suffers as a result (Jones Nat Bk v Yates 240 US 541). The borrower in these cases is still liable for the loan (Wilde v Amoretti Lodge Co 47 Wyo 505). A loan by a bank in which security has been omitted in violation of a statute is collectable. Since no officer has the right to impair the security of a bank, an agreement by an executive officer of the bank to postpone selling the collateral in case of default is ordinarily not binding on the bank (McBoyle v Union Nat Bk 162 Cal 277). A bank may make a loan in which it specifies that the obligation will become due before the date of maturity under certain contingencies, as with an installment loan that is defaulted (Morris Plan v Currie 161 NYS 292).

Discounting

Any advance charge for a loan, whether it is termed interest, premium or compensation, is a discount. Discounting is expressly granted by the National Bank Act, which states that a national bank shall have the power to discount and negotiate promissory notes, drafts, bills of exchange and other evidences of debt. The right to discount implies that all commercial banks may transfer negotiable notes that they hold (Evans v Nat Bk 251 US 108). So also a bank has the power to discount a draft with a bill of lading attached, nor is it liable to the consignee after he has paid the draft for any breach of the sales contract by the consignor-drawer of the draft (Hoffman v Nat City Bk 12 Wall (US) 181). Moreover, a bank that, as endorsee and innocent holder for value of a draft with bill of lading attached, collects it from the drawee is not bound to return the proceeds if the bill of lading proves to be forged (Spring v Hanove Nat Bk 209 NY 224).

Bank Liens

As a rule, banks have a general lien upon the securities of a customer or depositor that are in the bank's possession for credit advances made in the ordinary course of business (Garrison v Union T Co 139 Mich 392). A general lien does not apply to securities and collateral such as negotiable paper, stocks and bonds, mortgages and deeds, insurance policies and warehouse and similar receipts that are delivered to the bank for a particular transaction only. They cannot be used for payment for any claim but the one for which they are specifically pledged. Nor at the death of the customer may they be used against his general account (Reynes v Dumont 130 US 354). Except for a specific agreement to the contrary, commercial paper belonging to the customer deposited in the bank for collection is subject to the bank's lien enabling the bank to apply the proceeds to an indebtedness or general balance of the depositor's account. Bank liens may be forfeited by various agreements between the parties or by operation of law. They are not lost if the depositor becomes insolvent, makes an assignment for creditors and goes into the hands of a receiver (Joyce v Antin 179 US 591).

Set-offs

A bank has the right to a set-off against the general deposits for the payment of a debt due it by the depositor provided there is no agreement to the contrary. Rulings are numerous on this point. "Courts are justified in holding that a party by depositing funds with a bank," sums up a South Dakota decision, "authorizes the application of such funds to any overdraft or other indebtedness due from him to the bank" (Shotwell v Sioux Falls Savings Bk 34 SD 109). However, a bank may not set off against a deposit in the names of two persons a debt due from one of them unless the latter is shown to be the actual owner of the deposit (People's Bk of Denton v Turner 169 Ma 430).

Outside of an agreement, the bank may not set off an unmatured indebtedness of the depositor except where he has acted fraudulently (Gilmartin v Osborne T Co App 44 NYS2d 938). The law is unsettled as to the right of a bank to set off an unmatured indebtedness against a depositor's account that has been attached or garnished by a creditor.

Ordinarily, a bank has a right to apply a deposit towards its claims against the depositor even though he or his estate is insolvent, although a dissenting view holds that the appointment of a receiver or an assignee freezes the assets of the insolvent as of that date so that all creditors must share alike (Re Leon Keyser 98 NH 198). A bank that is liable as an endorser on the notes of a depositor may, on the insolvency of the latter, retain his deposits as an indemnity against his liability to pay (Citizens' Bk v Kendrick 92 Tenn 437). However, a bank has no legal duty to shift funds from the general deposit account of the maker of a note the bank holds to an endorser or guarantor when the note matures although there has been a ruling that if the bank knew the maker was insolvent it must exercise its right of set-off to protect the endorser and surety (Davenport v State Bkg Co 126 Ga 136). Opinion is divided as to whether or not a bank may charge a note it holds against a guarantor's checking account in the bank (Campbell v First Nat Bk 44 Fla 497). If a solvent depositor dies, the bank's right to set off its claims continues against his administrator or executor except for claims against the decedent not due at the time of his death (Laighton v Brookline T Co 225 Mass 458). If he is insolvent, some decisions allow claims against unmatured debts also.

Considerable conflict rages as to whether a bank must exhaust its collateral first before it can charge a depositor's indebtedness against his account (Prudential Realty Co v Allen 241 Mass 277). The right of set-off does not lie against deposits for a special and particular purpose only (Cassedy v Johnstown Bk 286 NYS 202). Nor may deposits of a person in trust for another have the depositor's individual debts charged against them (Boyle v Northwestern Nat Bk 125 Wis 498). A bank may waive its right of set-off by agreement or contract or even lose it by acts that estop it from claiming it (Joy v Grasse 173 Minn 289).

Overpayments

When a customer of a bank through a draft, check or order

draws more money from a bank than is charged to his account, the bank is entitled to recover the excess that is regarded as a loan to the depositor (Prowinsky v Second Nat Bk 49 App DC 363). If a bank permits an unauthorized agent to overdraw a depositor's account, it cannot secure the amount of the overdraft from the depositor unless restitution has been made to him. However, it can hold the principal liable if he has been concurring in the agent's practice by habitually paying his previous overdrafts (Merchants' & P Nat Bk v Clifton Mfg Co 56 SC 320). In general, the bank is supposed to know the condition of the depositor's account and if it makes a mistake in this respect it must take the consequences. If a bank cashes a check for a holder in due course mistakenly believing that the drawer has sufficient funds on deposit, in the absence of fraud, it can't recover from the payee. Nevertheless, many cases maintain that in spite of the bank's negligence, it may recover where the payee has not suffered damage as a result of the mistake (Manufacturers' T Co v Diamond 186 NYS 917). Although a drawee bank may not recover money paid on a check in the absence of funds, all rulings agree that payment in excess for which a particular check is drawn is always recoverable from the one to whom the payment was made (Kansas Lumber Co v Kansas Cent Bk 34 Kan 635).

Interest

Apparently, all early cultures had some doubts about the payment of interest. In Biblical times compensation for the use of money was considered unconscionable. Chinese and Hindus as well as the Koran prohibited the charging of excessive interest. The Mosaic Code barred Jews from taking interest from brethren but permitted it from Gentiles. The Romans allowed creditors to collect it from debtors for failure to pay. Its name derives from the Latin inter est, that which is "in between."

Interest is defined as "compensation allowed by law or fixed by the parties for the use of money or its equivalent" (Brown v Hiatt (US) 15 Wall 177). Simple interest is interest computed on the principal while compound interest is interest on interest. It is added to the principal. A distinction is drawn between the legal rate of interest that prevails when no special agreement has been made by the parties to a loan and the lawful rate of interest that is the maximum interest fixed by law. Usury consists of taking a rate of interest beyond the lawful rate (Evans v Nat Bk 251 US 108).

The rate of interest permitted is fixed by state law varying from state to state. In the absence of statute, any rate is legal (Houghton v Page 2 NH 42). Some states specifically ban taking interest beyond the legal rate, but others merely make an express provision for the allowance of interest. In the latter jurisdictions interest not authorized by law cannot be recovered unless actually contracted for (Totten v Totten 294 Ill 70).

A state law making provisions for different rates of interest for different kinds of borrowers is valid under the police power of the state if the classification of borrowers is reasonable. Statutes, for instance, exempting building and loan associations from the operation of the usury laws are not banned as class legislation because of the distinctive nature of their business (Cramer v Southern Ohio L & T Co 72 Ohio St 395). A statute may validly restrict the rate of interest that banks may charge on deposits (American Bkg & T Co v Boone 102 Ga 202), as well as the rates at which bank may discount notes so long as it applies to all banks (Youngblood v Birmingham T & S Co 95 Ala 121).

The National Bank Act permits national banks and their branches in foreign countries to charge the same rate of interest or discount as that authorized by the state or country in which they are situated. If no rate is fixed in these localities, national banks may charge a maximum rate of 1 percent in excess of the discount rate on ninety-day commercial paper in effect at their district Federal Reserve bank. However, state laws apply to national banks and they may not claim immunity from state regulations dealing with interest. A case arising in Georgia held that the maximum interest rate of 8 percent marked the limit that a national bank located there could charge in discounting (Evans v Nat Bk 251 US 108).

Usury

Under the usury laws the lender alone is considered the violator and suffers the consequences. Since the law of contracts governs interest agreements, usury is determined by the usury laws of the state in which the contract is executed. In many states, personal loan companies and industrial banking companies in some instances can charge up to 3 percent a month by special statute. In New York and many other states corporate debtors cannot plead usury as a defense nor is compound interest regarded as usurious although it is expressly forbidden in several states. The influential Chancellor Kent in an early nineteenth century decision voiced the legal attitude toward compounding "Interest upon interest, prompt and incessantly accruing could as a general rule become harsh and oppressive. Debt would accumulate with a rapidity beyond all calculation and endurance. Common business cannot sustain such overwhelming accumulation. It would tend to inflame and harden the heart of the creditor." (Connecticut v Jackson (NY) 1 Jone Ch 13). Although the law still does not favor compound interest, its attitude does not prevail in the face of a statute recognizing it (Penzer v Foster 170 Cal App 2d 106).

A transaction that assumes a certain form not to disguise usury but to avoid it is not necessarily usurious. So making a loan to a borrower and requiring that he keep some of it on deposit is not usurious if the entire sum is available at once to the borrower, but it is if the interest on the only part available to him exceeds the legal rate (Leonard v Coy 10 Neb 541). A transaction was considered usurious where part of a loan was retained as security by a finance company not only for the loan but also for all the other loans made by the borrower (Vee Bee Service v Household Finance Co 51 NYS 590).

On June 7, 1974, New York adopted a new law to lessen the use of "straw corporations"--dummies to avoid the usury laws--by providing that current laws that set chargeable maximum interest rates shall not apply to loans of $250,000 or more. If that sum is advanced in installments it will be considered a single loan for the amount. The law is not applicable to criminal usury.

Interest in Advance

Courts usually do not object to banks taking the entire amount of interest on a short-term loan in advance. However, when such an act boosted the rate of interest in excess of that specified as its lawful maximum, a finding of usury was sustained in a Kentucky case (Braurblett v Deposit Box Co 122 Ky 324). A national bank exacting more than the rate authorized by the state in which it was located may recover the principal sum even though the state's laws hold that usury bars the right to the principal (Stephens v Monongahela Nat Bk 88 Pa 157). However, such a bank purchasing negotiable paper knowing it to be void for usury has been prohibited from enforcing payment of it from its maker (Schlesinger v Lehmaier 191 NY 69). Under the National Bank Act, a bank that knowingly charges an illegal rate on a loan instrument makes the entire interest forfeit, not merely the excess covered by the instrument. Where the interest has been paid, the bank subjects itself to a penalty of twice the amount if an action for debt is started within two years of the time the usurious transaction occurred. This penalty may be exacted even if the state does not allow the recovery of usurious interest already paid (Barnett v Muncie Nat Bk 98 US 555).

Liability of Fiduciaries

The mere fact that a person administering an estate in the capacity of a trustee, administrator, executor or guardian deposits funds of the estate in a bank in which he owns a share does not make him liable for the interest on the deposit (Re Williams 55 Mont 63). However, if it is his private bank, he can be charged legal interest on the funds since he has commingled the property of the estate with his own (Re Brewster 113 Mich 561). If a bank or trust company acting as a fiduciary deposits or keeps funds it is administering, it is not liable for interest (First Nat Bk v Weaver 225 Ala 160) until further facts show that the funds have not been kept strictly separate (Triggs Savings & T Co v Triggs 330 Mass 324).

Appendix A

BANKING TERMS

Acceleration Clause--A clause in a loan agreement that makes the loan due and payable if any of the provisons are violated.

Acceptance--A draft or bill of exchange used in financing domestic and international trade in staple commodities. A trade acceptance is a draft drawn by the seller of goods on the buyer and accepted by the latter. In a bank acceptance a bank substitutes its own credit for its customer's credit and accepts drafts drawn under a letter of credit.

Accrued Interest--Interest owing but not yet paid.

Amortization--The process of extinguishing or reducing a debt by periodic payments sufficient to cover current interest and part of the principal.

Appraisal--An estimate of the value of property, especially real estate, presented as collateral for a loan.

Arbitrage--An operation in which foreign exchange is bought and sold simultaneously to make a profit from differences in prices.

Balance--The amount credited to the depositor's account that he is entitled to withdraw as well as the plus or minus difference between total debits and credits standing to the account of a bank at the clearing house.

Bank Draft--A check drawn by a bank against funds deposited to its account in another bank.

Bank Examiner--A representative of a state or federal bank supervisory agency who examines a bank's financial condition, management, and policies.

Bank Holding Company--A corporation organized under the laws of some states to engage in the acquisition of the stock of subsidiary commercial banks.

Bank Note--A promissory note issued by a bank payable to bearer on demand without interest and acceptable as money.

Bank Statement--A periodic statement showing a depositor all deposits recorded, checks paid and canceled, charges made, and balance left in his account.

Banker's Bill--A bill of exchange drawn by a bank on a foreign bank, sometimes called a banker's acceptance.

Bearer--A person holding a check, draft, bill, note or other instrument, especially if marked payable to bearer.

Beneficiary--a. The person specified by a depositor in an account for the credit of another or in trust for another.
b. The person designated to receive the income or principal of a trust estate.
c. The person who is to receive the proceeds of an insurance policy or an annuity.
d. The person in whose favor a letter of credit is issued.

Bill of Exchange--An unconditional written order requiring the person to whom it is addressed to pay on demand or at a fixed time a sum certain in money to order or to bearer.

Bond--An interest-bearing certificate of debt that promises under seal that the issuer, usually a government or a corporation, will pay the amount of the bond to its holder at a specified date.

Brokered Funds--Money solicited by banks from money brokers to increase the lending capacity of their banks.

Call Money--Money loaned by banks, usually to stock exchange brokers, for which demand may be made at any time.

Capital Funds--The total of the capital accounts of a bank, including the total stated or par value of the capital stock, surplus, undivided profits, and capital reserves, as well as any other proprietary claims.

Cash Items--Items, usually checks or coupons, accepted for tentative credit to a depositor's account, subject to rejection if the items are not paid.

Cashier's Check--A check drawn by a bank upon its own funds and signed by an authorized officer.

Certificate of Deposit--A written acknowledgment by a bank of a deposit payable upon the return of the certificate on a specified date. The deposit is usually interest-bearing and may not be withdrawn in any way before maturity.

Certification--A stamped and signed assurance by a bank on which a check is drawn that sufficient funds are on deposit to cover the check.

Chain Banking--The control of two or more banks by individuals rather than by a corporation or similar company.

Check--A bill of exchange drawn on a checking account payable on demand.

Checking Account--A bank account against which checks may be drawn.

Clearing--A system whereby banks offset claims and counter-claims for checks and other items held against each other so that only balances need be settled.

Clearinghouse--A place where representatives of commercial banks in the same locality get together to do their clearing and settle the resulting balances.

Collateral--A pledge of specific property as security for repayment of a loan at a certain time. It can be sold if the loan is defaulted.

Collection Items--Drafts, notes acceptances, and other items received by a bank that must be collected before proceeds can be credited to a depositor's account.

Comaker--One who signs the note of another, either for value or accommodation. In either situation he is liable to the payee.

Commercial Bank--Commercial banks accept and hold demand deposits, which provide excess reserves to extend credit to borrowing customers, creating money in the process. Although they accept time and savings deposits, their essential and unique function is to deal with demand deposits.

Commercial Paper--All sorts of short-term negotiable instruments stemming from business transactions.

Compound Interest--Interest upon principal plus accrued interest.

Consumer Credit--Loans and sale credit extended to individuals to finance the purchase of goods and services arising out of consumer needs and desires.

Correspondent Bank--A bank that carries a deposit balance with another bank or maintains reciprocal services with a bank in another city.

Countersign--The addition of a signature to an instrument to attest its authenticity.

Credit--An advance of cash, merchandise, service, or something of value in the present in return for a promise to pay for it at some future date, usually with an agreed interest. If the credit period is less than a year, it is called short-term. Over that it may be called intermediate or long-term, depending on the length of the credit period. Long-term credit for over five years is often obtained in the sale of stocks, bonds or mortgages.

Credit Union--A cooperative association whose members pool their savings by purchasing shares. Lending is not for home building but for other personal needs.

Currency--Generally used to describe paper money, it includes coin, government notes, and bank notes in circulation as a medium of exchange.

Demand Deposit--Funds in a checking account subject to withdrawal on demand.

Discount--A discount transaction is one where interest is deducted from the principal amount of a loan at the time the credit is arranged.

Dividends--A stockholder's share in the earnings of his company. In mutual savings banks and savings and loan associations, a specified percentage of the net earnings distributed to depositors.

Draft--A written order signed by the drawer directing the drawee to pay a specified sum of money to the payee or his order.

Eligible Paper--Negotiable notes qualified for discount and purchase by a central bank.

Endorsement or Indorsement--Endorsement is the technical act of signing one's name without qualifications to the bank of a negotiable instrument for the purpose of transfer.

Escheat--The reversion of unclaimed deposits in a bank to the state.

Escrow--An escrow holds something of value for one person that is to be delivered to another upon the fulfillment of a specified contingency agreed upon between the parties. A bank often acts as a depository for the property involved.

Exchange Charge--A charge imposed by banks for certain exchange services, such as for drafts on banks in other cities or for collecting out of town items.

Exchanges--Items on banks presented for collection in a regional clearing house.

Federal Funds--Excess deposits and claims against such deposits kept by commercial banks, the United States Treasury, and others at Federal Reserve banks, which can be borrowed, usually for a single day at minimum cost by banks to improve their reserve balances.

Fiduciary--One who acts in a capacity of trust or confidence for another as executor of an estate, receiver in bankruptcy, guardian of an infant or insane person, trustee under a will, or similar position.

Float--Items in transit not yet collected.

Foreclose--To bar a mortgagor from redeeming mortgaged property.

Guaranty--An undertaking to answer for the payment of a debt or performance of a duty in the event of another's default.

Holder in Due Course--One who has taken an instrument, complete and regular on its face, before it was overdue, in good faith and for value, without notice of any infirmity in the instrument or defect in the title of the person negotiating it.

Honor--To accept or pay an item when presented. The opposite is to dishonor.

Indemnity--A security against hurt, loss, or damage.

Indirect Liability--A secondary liability assumed by an endorser or guarantor of an obligation for which someone else is primarily liable.

Interest--The sum paid for the use of money or credit.

Joint Account--An account in the name of two or more persons.

Kiting--Writing checks for amounts in excess of funds in a checking account. The drawer takes advantage of the time needed by the bank to collect the checks. The term also refers to altering a check by raising the amount.

Letter of Credit--An instrument issued by a commercial bank to an individual or corporation in which the bank substitutes its own credit for that of the individual or corporation.

Liquidity--The capability of quick conversion of assets into cash.

Loan--The grant of a temporary use of money by a lender to be repaid later, usually with interest.

Maker--The person who executes a note or other promise to pay. Drawer and maker are often interchangeable terms.

Maturity--The due date of a mortgage, bond, stock, draft, or similar instrument.

Money Order--A draft sold by a bank for a fee. A Postal Money Order is sold by the post office.

Mortgage--A pledge of property for debt in which the lender (mortgagee) may foreclose the security if the debtor (mortgagor) fails to meet the terms of the contract.

Negotiable Instrument--An unconditional but transferable written order or promise to pay money by the drawer to order or to bearer or drawee at a determinable time.

Nonpar Banks--Banks that deduct an exchange charge before remitting an item to a collecting bank. Federal Reserve banks will collect items only from par banks.

No Protest--A waiver of formal protest of a negotiable instrument, which is also deemed to be a waiver of presentment and notice of dishonor.

Open Market Operations--The activities of the Federal Reserve in buying and selling certain types of securities in the open market both here and abroad as part of its credit and monetary stabilization policy.

Overdraft--The amount owing to a bank that has paid an item drawn against insufficient funds.

Par Value--Fixed value exclusive of interest of a stock or bond or similar obligation for the payment of money printed on the certificate.

Passbook--A book furnished by the bank in which the depositor keeps a record of his account. A savings bank passbook contains a record of deposits, withdrawals, and interest credited.

Postdated Check--A check dated ahead. It is not payable until the date specified.

Prime Rate--Preferential rate of interest on loans given to large and regular borrowers by banks.

Principal--The face amount of a note or other evidence of debt on which interest is figured.

Promissory Note--A written promise by the maker to pay a certain sum of money to the payee or his order on demand or on a fixed date.

Protest--A written certification, usually by a notary, that he has presented a negotiable instrument and that the instrument was dishonored by refusal to accept or pay. Unless waived, an obligation involving a party in a second state or foreign country must be protested in order to hold endorsers responsible in the event of nonpayment.

Raised Check--A check in which the amount has been fraudulently increased.

Rediscount--A discount of commercial paper for a second time by one bank or another. The negotiation of a note by an endorser is rediscounting. Federal Reserve District banks rediscount for member banks.

Redlining--The red-penciling of local maps by lenders in order to delete a section of the city from its approved investment areas.

Regulation Q--The Federal Reserve ruling regulating the rate of interest banks may pay.

Reserves--Funds set aside by a bank to enable it to pay its depositors in cash on demand. Reserves may consist of cash in the vault, demand deposits in other banks, or legal reserves deposited with the bank's district Federal Reserve bank.

Return Item--An item returned unpaid by a payor bank.

Run on a Bank--Persistent and heavy withdrawals of cash from a bank, usually caused by doubts of the bank's safety.

Safe Deposit Box--A place rented by a customer to keep valuables to which he only has access.

Securities--The general name for stocks, mortgages, bonds, coupons, or certificates evidencing ownership or creditorship in a corporation or property.

Service Charge--Fee charged to depositors for various services of banks, such as for checks and their use, the issuance of money orders and drafts or the safekeeping of securities.

Sight Draft--A bill of exchange or draft payable on presentation. A foreign exchange sight draft is a check stated in foreign currency in a foreign bank drawn against the balance maintained in that bank by the seller of the draft.

Signature--A signature includes symbol, trade name, or any word or mark. It may be with pencil, ink, crayon, or any means to record a signature or figures, or a mark may be used in lieu of the proper name and a party intending may bind himself effectively by using such. In a bank, the depositor's signature must correspond with that on his signature card.

Straight Paper--Notes that are the obligation of one party only--the maker.

Stale Check--One that is kept a long time before presentation to the bank for cashing. It can be refused.

Stop Payment Order--An order by a depositor to his bank to refuse payment of an item specified by him.

Surety Company--A firm that insures against losses due generally to failure of someone to perform a job contracted for. It issues all kinds of bonds including bankers' bonds covering all types of losses.

Survivorship Account--An account in the name of two or more persons which on the death of one belongs to the survivor or survivors.

Teller's Check--A bank draft signed by the teller of the drawer bank often given for money withdrawn from a savings bank.

Term-loan--A loan to business firm repayable after the lapse of a year or more.

Time Deposit--Deposits withdrawable at a specified future date or after the lapse of a specific period of time or upon thirty or more days of advance notice of withdrawal.

Transit Items--Cash items payable outside the city of the bank receiving them for credit to the customer's account and sent by mail to a payor bank by a collecting bank.

Traveler's Checks--Checks issued by banks and express companies promising to pay on demand even amounts of money. The buyer signs the check on purchase and countersigns it for payment.

Ultra Vires Act--An act beyond the legal power or authority of the performer.

Usury--Interest in excess of the legal rate charged to a borrower for the use of money.

Appendix B
FEDERAL RESERVE SYSTEM

Source: Statistical Abstract of the United States, 1974; Department of Commerce, Social and Economic Statistics Administration, Bureau of the Census, pp. 450, 451, 464

1. **Federal Reserve Bank of New York—Discount Rates: 1955 to 1974**

[Percent per year. See also *Historical Statistics, Colonial Times to 1957*, series X 312-313]

EFFECTIVE DATE	RATE	EFFECTIVE DATE	RATE	EFFECTIVE DATE	RATE
1955—Apr. 15	1¾	1960—June 10	3½	1971—Jan. 8	5¼
Aug. 5	2	Aug. 12	3	Jan. 22	5
Sept. 9	2¼	1963—July 17	3½	Feb. 19	4¾
Nov. 18	2½	1964—Nov. 24	4	July 16	5
1956—Apr. 13	2¾	1965—Dec. 6	4½	Nov. 19	4¾
Aug. 24	3	1967—Apr. 7	4	Dec. 17	4½
1957—Aug. 23	3½	Nov. 20	4½		
Nov. 15	3			1973—Jan. 15	5
1958—Jan. 24	2¾	1968—Mar. 22	5	Feb. 26	5½
Mar. 7	2¼	Apr. 19	5½	May 4	5¾
Apr. 18	1¾	Aug. 30	5¼	May 11	6
Sept. 12	2	Dec. 18	5½	June 11	6½
Nov. 7	2½	1969—Apr. 4	6	July 2	7
1959—Mar. 6	3	1970—Nov. 13	5¾	Aug. 14	7½
May 29	3½	Dec. 4	5½		
Sept. 11	4			In effect Apr. 30, 1974	8

2. Federal Reserve System—Maximum Interest Rates Payable on Time and Savings Deposits: 1962 to 1974

[**Percent per year.** Maximum rates payable by Federal Reserve member banks; may not exceed maximum rates payable by State banks or trust companies on like deposits under laws of State where member bank is located]

TYPE OF DEPOSIT	Jan. 1962	July 1963	Nov. 1964	Dec. 1965	July 1966	Sept. 1966	Apr. 1968	Jan. 1970–June 1973	July 1973–Jan. 1974
Savings	[1] 4	[1] 4	4	4	4	4	4	4½	5
Multiple maturity:									
90 days or more					5	5	5	[2] 5–5¾	(4)
Less than 90 days (30–89 days)	[3] 4	[3] 4	[3] 4½	[3] 5½	4	4	4	4½	
Single maturity:									
Less than $100,000					5½	5	5	[5] 5–5¾	[6] 5–7¼
$100,000 or more					5½	5½	[7] 5½–6¼	[8] 6¼–7½	(9)

[1] 3½ percent for deposits of less than 12 months maturity.

[2] 5 percent, 90 days to 1 year; 5½ percent, 1 to 2 years; 5¾ percent, 2 years and over.

[3] Prior to July 20, 1966, time deposits other than savings were not segregated as to multiple or single maturity or by denomination. Rates shown for Dec. 1965 are for all maturities of 30 days or more; rates for July 1963 and Nov. 1964 are for deposits with maturities of 90 days or more, and for Jan. 1962 for maturities of 12 months or more; for rates applicable to shorter maturities, see *Annual Report* of the U.S. Board of Governors of the Federal Reserve System, 1970, p. 232.

[4] Effective July 16, 1973, the distinction between single- and multiple-maturity deposits was eliminated.

[5] 5 percent, 30 days to 1 year; 5½ percent, 1 to 2 years; 5¾ percent, 2 years and over.

[6] 5 percent, 30–89 days; 5½ percent 90 days to 1 year; 6 percent, 1 to 2½ years; 6½ percent, 2½ years or more except for 4 year deposits in minimum denominations of $1,000 which had no ceiling between July and November, 1973. Effective November 1, 1973, a ceiling of 7¼ percent was imposed on 4-year deposits.

[7] 5½ percent, 30–59 days; 5¾ percent, 60–89 days; 6 percent, 90–179 days; 6¼ percent, 180 days and over.

[8] 6¼ percent, 30–59 days; 6½ percent, 60–89 days; 6¾ percent, 90–179 days; 7 percent, 180 days to 1 year; 7½ percent, 1 year or more. Effective June 24, 1970, maximum interest rates on maturities of less than 90 days were suspended.

[9] Maximum interest rates on time deposits of $100,000 or more were suspended: Effective June 1970, on maturities of less than 90 days, effective May 1973, on maturities of 90 days or more.

Source of tables: Board of Governors of the Federal Reserve System, *Federal Reserve Bulletin*, monthly.

3. FEDERAL RESERVE BANKS—ASSETS, LIABILITIES, AND CAPITAL ACCOUNTS: 1950 TO 1973

[In millions of dollars. As of December 31. See also Historical Statistics, Colonial Times to 1957, series X 245-254]

ITEM	1950	1955	1960	1965	1970	1971	1972	1973
Total assets or liabilities and capital accounts	47,172	52,340	52,984	62,652	85,913	94,595	94,765	103,272
Assets:								
U.S. Government securities [1]	20,778	24,785	27,384	40,768	62,142	70,804	71,220	80,495
Gold certificate reserves	21,456	21,009	17,479	13,436	10,457	9,875	10,303	11,460
Special drawing rights	(X)	(X)	(X)	(X)	400	400	400	400
Cash and collection items	4,537	6,188	7,698	7,044	11,899	12,148	9,495	8,439
Loans and acceptances	67	136	107	324	392	300	2,087	1,326
Other assets	333	222	317	1,080	1,123	1,068	1,260	1,152
Liabilities and capital:								
Federal Reserve notes	23,587	26,921	28,449	37,074	50,323	53,819	58,757	64,262
Deposits	19,810	20,355	18,336	19,620	28,687	31,101	28,667	31,486
Deferred availability cash items	2,902	3,917	4,941	4,667	6,917	7,344	5,199	4,805
Other, and accrued dividends	6	15	31	189	582	647	557	981
Capital accounts	869	1,132	1,226	1,102	1,404	1,484	1,586	1,688

- Represents zero.   X Not applicable.   [1] Beginning 1970, includes securities loaned—fully secured by U.S. Government securities pledged with Federal Reserve banks.

4. FEDERAL RESERVE SYSTEM—MEMBER BANK RESERVES: 1950 TO 1973

[In millions of dollars. As of December; averages of daily figures]

ITEM	1950	1955	1960	1965	1970	1971	1972	1973
Factors supplying reserve funds:								
F.R. bank credit outstanding [1]	21,606	26,853	29,060	43,853	66,708	74,254	76,851	85,642
U.S. Government securities [2]	20,345	24,602	27,248	40,885	61,688	69,158	71,094	79,701
Float	1,117	1,389	1,665	2,349	3,570	3,905	3,479	3,414
Other F.R. assets	142	840	94	490	1,353	1,099	2,187	2,377
Gold stock	22,879	21,689	17,954	13,799	11,105	10,132	10,410	11,567
Special drawing rights certificate account	(X)	(X)	(X)	(X)	400	400	400	400
Treasury currency outstanding	4,629	5,008	5,396	5,565	7,145	7,614	8,293	8,668
Factors absorbing reserve funds:								
Currency in circulation	27,806	31,265	33,019	42,206	57,013	61,063	66,060	71,646
Treasury cash holdings	1,290	777	408	808	427	453	850	323
Deposits with F.R. banks [3]	1,888	1,287	1,267	1,068	1,729	2,944	2,852	3,015
Other F.R. accounts	739	983	1,029	389	2,285	2,287	2,362	2,942
Member bank reserves	17,391	19,240	19,283	22,719	29,265	31,329	[4]31,853	[4]35,068
With F.R. banks	17,391	19,240	16,688	18,747	23,925	25,653	24,830	28,352
Currency and coin [5]	-	-	2,595	3,972	5,340	5,676	6,095	6,635
Required reserves	16,364	18,646	18,527	22,267	28,993	31,164	31,134	34,806
Excess reserves	1,027	594	756	452	272	165	[4]219	262
Free reserves [6]	885	-245	669	-2	-49	58	-530	-1,036

X Not applicable. [1] Includes industrial loans and acceptances, when held.
[2] Includes Federal agency obligations. [3] Other than member bank reserves.
[4] Includes $428 million for 1972 and $81 million for 1973 of reserve deficiencies of which Federal Reserve Banks are allowed to waive penalties for a transition period. [5] Beginning 1965, figures are estimates. [6] Excess less borrowings.

5. FEDERAL RESERVE SYSTEM, ALL MEMBER BANKS—INCOME, EXPENSES, AND DIVIDENDS: 1950 TO 1973

[Money figures in millions of dollars; ratios in percentages. Prior to 1960, excludes all member banks in Alaska (except for one bank in 1955) and Hawaii; beginning 1960, includes one member bank in the Virgin Islands]

ITEM	1950	1955	1960	1965	1970 [1]	1971	1972	1973
Number of banks	6,873	6,543	6,174	6,221	5,767	5,727	5,704	5,735
Current revenue	3,255	5,343	8,928	13,842	27,913	28,670	31,335	41,708
Expenses	2,020	3,265	5,655	10,206	22,193	23,346	25,639	35,027
Net current earnings	1,245	2,077	3,273	3,636	5,720	5,325	5,696	6,681
Net income	781	985	1,689	2,103	3,823	4,117	4,400	5,012
Cash dividends declared	346	501	735	1,058	1,754	1,908	1,839	2,018
Capital accounts [2]	9,455	12,499	16,710	24,060	33,111	35,734	39,322	43,023
Ratios to average capital accounts:								
Net current earnings	13.2	16.6	19.6	15.1	17.3	14.9	14.5	15.5
Net income	8.3	7.9	10.1	8.7	11.5	11.5	11.2	11.7
Cash dividends declared	3.7	4.0	4.4	4.4	5.3	5.3	4.7	4.7

[1] Not comparable with prior years.   [2] Averages of amounts reported for varying call dates; for details, see source.

Source of tables: Board of Governors of the Federal Reserve System, *Federal Reserve Bulletin*, monthly.

6. FEDERAL RESERVE SYSTEM—MEMBER BANK RESERVE REQUIREMENTS: 1972 TO 1974

[Percent of deposits. Effective Nov. 9, 1972, a new criterion was adopted to designate reserve cities. The presence of a Federal Reserve Bank or branch or of the head office of a bank having net demand deposits of more than $400 million constitutes designation of that place as a reserve city bank. Any banks, wherever located, having net demand deposits of $400 million or less are considered banks outside of reserve cities and are permitted to maintain reserves at ratios set for banks not in reserve cities]

EFFECTIVE DATE OF CHANGE	NET DEMAND DEPOSITS [1]						TIME DEPOSITS [2]			
	Under $2 million	$2 million to $10 million	$10 million to $100 million	$100 million to $400 million	$400 million and over	Savings	Other time		
							$5 million and under	Over $5 million	
1972—Nov. 9	8	10	12	4 16½	17½	3	3	5	
Nov. 16	8	10	12	13	17½	3	3	5	
1973—July 19	8	10½	12½	13½	18	3	3	5	
In effect Apr. 30, 1974	8	10½	12½	13½	18	3	3	5	

	Minimum	Maximum
Legal requirements as of Apr. 30, 1974:		
Net demand deposits, reserve city banks	10	22
Net demand deposits, other banks	7	14
Time deposits	3	10

[1] Demand deposits subject to reserve requirements are gross demand deposits minus cash items in process of collection and demand balances due from domestic banks. [2] Reserve city banks. [3] Christmas and vacation club accounts subject to same requirements as savings deposits. [4] Applied only to former reserve city banks for one week. Other banks continued previous requirement of 13 percent.

Source: Board of Governors of the Federal Reserve System, *Federal Reserve Bulletin*, monthly.

7.

Source: Code of Federal Regulations, Volume 12, Banks and Banking (12 CFR 329.6, 329.7.)

§ 329.6 Maximum rates of interest payable on time and savings deposits by insured nonmember banks other than insured nonmember mutual savings banks.[13]

(a) Deposits of $100,000 or more. There is no maximum rate of interest presently prescribed on any time deposit of $100,000 or more.

(b) Deposits of less than $100,000. (1) Except as provided in paragraph (b) (2) of this section, no insured nonmember bank shall pay interest on any time deposit of less than $100,000 at a rate in excess of the applicable rate under the following schedule:

Maturity	Maximum percent per annum
30 days or more but less than 90 days	5
90 days or more but less than 1 year	5-1/2
1 year or more but less than 30 months	6
30 months or more	6-1/2

(2) Deposits of $1,000 or more with maturities of 4 years or more. No insured nonmember bank shall pay interest on any time deposit of $1,000 or more with a maturity of four years or more at a rate in excess of 7-1/4 percent per annum.

(c) Savings deposits. No insured nonmember bank shall pay interest at a rate in excess of 5 percent per annum on any savings deposit, including savings deposits that are subject to withdrawal by negotiable or transferable instruments for the purpose of making transfers to third parties.

[38 FR 20247, July 30, 1973, as amended at 38 FR 20818, Aug. 3, 1973; 38 FR 29315, Oct. 24, 1973; 38 FR 34458, Dec. 14, 1973]

§ 329.7 Maximum rate of interest or dividends payable on deposits by insured nonmember mutual savings banks.[14]

(a) Definition. For the purposes of this section, the term "mutual savings bank" includes any mutual savings bank and any

[13] The maximum rates of interest payable by insured nonmember banks on time and savings deposits as prescribed herein are not applicable to any deposit which is payable only at an office of an insured nonmember bank located outside of the States of the United States and the District of Columbia.

[14] The maximum rates of interest payable by insured nonmember

guaranty savings bank which operates in the State of New Hampshire substantially under and pursuant to the laws of that State pertaining to mutual savings banks so long as such guaranty savings bank does not engage in commercial banking.

(b) Maximum rates payable--(1) General.--(i) Except as provided in paragraphs (b) (2), (3) and (4) and paragraph (e) of this section, no insured nonmember mutual savings bank shall pay interest or dividends at a rate in excess of 5-1/4 percent per annum on any deposit. Section 329.3(b), relating to modification of deposit contracts to conform to regulations, shall apply to insured nonmember mutual savings banks.

(ii) Notwithstanding the provisions of paragraph (b) (1) (i) of this section, no insured nonmember mutual savings bank shall pay interest or dividends at a rate in excess of 5 percent per annum on any deposit that is subject to withdrawal by negotiable or transferable instruments for the purpose of making transfers to third parties where such withdrawals are authorized by law.[14a] Those eligible to hold such deposits shall be limited to individuals and those organizations described in Section 329.1 (e) (1) (i).

(2) Time deposits of $100,000 or more. There is no maximum rate of interest or dividends presently prescribed on any time deposit of $100,000 or more.

(3) Time deposits of less than $100,000. Except as provided in paragraph (b) (4) of this section, no insured nonmember mutual savings bank shall pay interest or dividends on any time deposit of less than $100,000 at a rate in excess of the applicable rate under the following schedule:

Maturity	Maximum percent per annum
90 days or more but less than 1 year-----------	5-3/4
1 year or more but less than 30 months---------	6-1/2
30 months or more-------------------------------	6-3/4

mutual savings banks as prescribed herein are not applicable to any deposit which is payable only at an office of an insured nonmember mutual savings bank located outside of the States of the United States and the District of Columbia.

[14a] Federal law limits the offering of such deposits by mutual savings banks to those banks located in Massachusetts and New Hampshire .(87 Stat. 342).

(4) Time deposits of $1,000 or more with maturities of 4 years or more. No insured nonmember mutual savings bank shall pay interest or dividends on any time deposit of $1,000 or more with a maturity of four years or more at a rate in excess of 7-1/2 percent per annum.

(c) Compounding interest. In determining the maximum amount of interest or dividends permitted to be paid, the effects of compounding may be disregarded.

(d) Grace periods in computing interest. An insured nonmember mutual savings bank may pay interest or dividends on a deposit received during the first 10 calendar days of any calendar month at the applicable maximum rate prescribed in paragraph (b) of this section calculated from the first day of such calendar month until such deposit is withdrawn or otherwise ceases to constitute a deposit upon which interest or dividends are payable; and an insured nonmember mutual savings bank may pay interest or dividends on a deposit withdrawn during the last 3 business days of any calendar month ending a regular quarterly or semi-annual interest or dividend period at the applicable maximum rate prescribed in paragraph (b) of this section calculated to the end of such calendar month.

(e) Systematic savings account deposits in insured nonmember mutual savings banks in Massachusetts. No insured nonmember mutual savings bank located in the Commonwealth of Massachusetts shall pay interest or dividends on any systematic savings account deposit, as defined in section 22B of chapter 168 of the General Laws of the Commonwealth of Massachusetts, at a rate in excess of the applicable rate under the following schedule:

Minimum period	Maximum percent per annum
48 months	5-1/2
96 months	5-3/4

(f) Time deposits. The provisions of this Part 329 with respect to time deposits, except the provisions of § 329.6, shall apply to all such deposits in insured nonmember mutual savings banks.

Appendix C
COMMERCIAL BANKS

Source: Statistical Abstract of the United States, 1974;
Department of Commerce, Social and Economic Statistics Administration, Bureau of the Census, pp. 452, 453, 454, 455.

1. COMMERCIAL BANKS—ASSETS, LIABILITIES, AND CAPITAL ACCOUNTS: 1950 TO 1973

[Money figures in billions of dollars. As of December 31. Includes nondeposit trust companies. Includes Puerto Rico and outlying areas. Beginning 1965, includes asset and liability figures for branches of foreign banks (tabulated as banks) licensed to do a deposit business. See *Historical Statistics, Colonial Times to 1967*, series X 97–118 for related data]

ITEM	1950	1955	1960	1965	1970	1971	1972	1973
Number of banks	14,164	13,756	13,484	13,818	13,705	13,804	13,950	14,194
Assets	170.5	213.1	260.7	382.9	581.5	646.3	746.1	842.9
Loans and securities	128.0	163.0	202.5	311.5	465.1	520.9	604.0	689.4
Investment securities 1	74.8	78.6	82.0	104.6	142.7	165.0	180.0	181.2
U.S. Treasury	62.3	61.9	61.1	59.7	59.3	63.0	65.1	55.7
Obligations of States and subdivisions	8.2	12.8	17.6	38.7	67.9	80.6	87.9	91.8
Other	4.3	4.0	3.3	6.2	15.6	21.4	27.0	33.7
Trading account securities	–	–	–	–	5.7	5.3	5.2	8.7
Federal funds sold and securities purchased under agreements to resell	–	–	–	2.1	16.3	20.0	26.7	35.4
Other loans and discounts	53.2	84.4	120.5	204.7	300.4	330.6	392.1	464.1
Commercial and industrial loans	22.0	33.4	43.4	71.9	113.4	119.6	134.1	160.8
Real estate loans	13.7	21.0	28.8	49.7	73.3	82.5	99.3	119.1
Secured by farmland	1.0	1.3	1.6	2.9	4.4	4.2	4.8	5.4
Secured by residential properties	10.4	15.9	20.4	32.4	45.6	52.0	62.8	74.9
Secured by other properties	2.3	3.8	6.8	14.4	23.3	26.3	31.7	38.7

Loans to domestic commercial and foreign banks	.1	.6	1.0	2.2	2.7	4.6	6.7	10.3
Loans to other financial institutions	(²)	(²)	7.1	13.3	15.9	17.1	23.5	30.7
Loans to brokers and dealers in securities	1.8	3.3	3.3	5.3	6.3	7.3	11.3	7.7
Other securities loans	1.1	1.8	1.8	3.2	3.5	3.7	4.5	4.3
Loans to farmers (excluding real estate)	2.9	4.5	5.7	8.2	11.2	12.5	14.3	17.3
Other loans to individuals	10.2	17.3	26.5	45.7	66.3	75.1	88.0	100.8
All other loans (including overdrafts)	1.5	2.6	2.9	5.3	7.7	8.2	10.3	13.3
Cash, balances with banks, collection items	40.4	47.0	52.2	61.0	94.0	100.3	113.8	119.2
Currency and coin	2.2	2.7	3.4	4.9	7.1	7.6	8.7	10.8
Balances with banks, including reserve	28.5	31.0	30.6	33.6	47.1	54.0	59.6	63.7
Cash items in process of collection	9.7	13.3	18.3	22.5	39.8	38.7	45.5	44.8
Bank premises, furniture, fixtures	1.3	1.9	3.2	5.2	9.6	10.7	11.6	12.8
Other	.8	1.2	2.7	5.2	12.8	14.4	16.7	21.3
Liabilities, reserves, capital accounts	170.5	213.1	260.7	382.9	581.5	646.3	746.1	842.9
Deposits	156.1	193.2	230.5	333.8	486.5	542.9	621.5	687.6
Demand	118.8	142.5	156.8	185.5	249.0	264.1	298.6	311.7
Time	37.3	50.7	73.7	148.5	236.5	278.6	322.9	375.9
Business and personal	129.4	159.6	189.0	276.8	397.3	442.1	507.4	558.7
Government	12.6	16.9	22.6	32.4	49.7	59.3	67.9	73.9
Domestic interbank	12.3	13.8	15.8	17.5	29.2	32.4	34.0	38.0
Foreign government and bank	1.8	2.9	3.1	7.0	9.3	9.2	12.3	16.9
Miscellaneous liabilities	2.1	3.2	6.8	14.7	46.5	49.4	64.7	89.0
Reserves on loans and securities	.7	1.3	2.4	4.0	6.3	6.5	6.9	7.8
Capital accounts	11.7	15.4	21.1	30.4	43.2	47.5	52.9	58.4
Capital notes and debentures	—	—	—	1.7	2.2	3.1	4.2	4.2
Equity capital	11.6	15.4	21.0	28.7	41.0	44.4	48.7	54.2
Stock	3.6	4.7	6.3	8.7	11.4	12.0	13.0	14.0
Surplus	5.3	7.3	10.0	13.6	18.2	20.4	21.7	23.7
Undivided profits and reserves	2.7	3.4	4.7	6.4	11.4	12.4	14.0	16.5

- Represents zero. ¹ Prior to 1970, securities were reported on a net (after deduction of reserves) basis in total assets. ² Not available separately; included in commercial loans and other loans.

Source: U.S. Federal Deposit Insurance Corporation, *Assets and Liabilities: Commercial and Mutual Savings Banks*, semiannual.

2.   COMMERCIAL BANKS—NUMBER, BANKING OFFICES, ASSETS, AND DEPOSITS, BY CLASS OF BANK: 1970 AND 1973

[Money figures in billions of dollars. As of December 31]

CLASS OF BANK	BANKS		BANKING OFFICES		ASSETS		DEMAND DEPOSITS		TIME DEPOSITS	
	1970	1973	1970	1973	1970	1973	1970	1973	1970	1973
All banks	13,666	14,171	35,531	40,624	577.0	835.7	247.9	310.1	233.9	372.3
National	4,621	4,659	17,157	19,575	340.8	489.5	145.1	179.0	138.6	216.8
State member	1,147	1,076	4,802	5,126	125.5	166.8	58.5	66.6	43.0	64.8
Insured nonmember	7,735	8,229	13,139	15,671	106.5	170.8	42.5	62.0	51.5	88.2
Noninsured	184	207	433	252	4.4	8.7	1.7	2.4	.9	2.6

Source: Board of Governors of the Federal Reserve System, *Federal Reserve Bulletin*, monthly.

3. INSURED COMMERCIAL BANKS—ASSETS AND LIABILITIES, STATES AND OTHER AREAS: 1973

[Money figures in millions of dollars. As of December 31]

STATE OR OTHER AREA	Number of banks	Total assets or liabilities	SELECTED ASSETS			Capital accounts	SELECTED LIABILITIES		
			Loans and discounts	Securities	Cash, bank balances and collection items		Total	Deposits	
								Demand	Time
Total	13,976	832,661	459,783	222,606	116,936	57,838	681,620	309,104	372,515
United States	13,964	827,063	456,220	221,886	116,262	57,603	677,358	307,632	369,725
Alabama	287	8,997	4,588	3,011	1,133	682	7,712	3,555	4,166
Alaska	10	920	464	303	110	65	795	347	448
Arizona	15	7,057	4,385	408	873	400	5,785	2,225	3,560
Arkansas	254	5,677	2,812	1,873	845	410	4,922	2,410	2,512
California	174	88,157	51,899	19,967	11,881	4,933	70,849	28,060	42,789
Colorado	255	7,822	4,398	1,885	1,243	531	6,629	3,337	3,292
Connecticut	67	7,966	4,677	1,786	1,206	566	6,871	3,696	3,175
Delaware	18	2,256	1,142	835	203	165	1,787	911	876
District of Columbia	15	4,067	2,182	1,177	588	323	3,437	1,997	1,440
Florida	642	26,347	12,671	9,111	3,747	1,891	22,855	10,903	12,052
Georgia	432	14,454	8,452	3,209	2,110	1,099	11,143	5,789	5,354
Hawaii	8	2,680	1,693	665	313	185	2,384	993	1,361
Idaho	24	2,434	1,438	598	317	150	2,160	921	1,239
Illinois	1,105	63,796	35,667	18,921	6,863	4,226	51,828	20,332	31,494
Indiana	407	18,261	9,349	6,188	2,214	1,175	15,342	6,368	8,974
Iowa	661	10,980	5,514	3,927	1,317	795	9,549	3,990	5,554
Kansas	611	8,574	3,970	3,221	1,163	694	7,344	3,588	3,756
Kentucky	341	9,193	4,579	3,176	1,189	661	7,829	3,898	3,931
Louisiana	244	11,748	5,804	3,944	1,641	829	9,720	4,510	5,209
Maine	44	2,005	1,274	452	210	150	1,744	715	1,029
Maryland	112	8,888	5,154	2,410	1,072	671	7,535	3,688	3,851

Massachusetts	148	17,550	9,912	4,229	2,600	1,279	14,098	8,013	6,085
Michigan	338	31,027	18,458	8,438	3,822	2,194	26,923	9,335	17,588
Minnesota	737	15,616	8,242	5,189	1,745	1,056	12,657	5,085	7,572
Mississippi	181	5,610	2,878	1,782	797	399	2,657	2,361	2,854
Missouri	681	18,378	8,724	6,727	2,428	1,379	15,042	7,785	7,256
Montana	149	2,735	1,496	873	295	182	2,396	934	1,462
Nebraska	444	6,302	3,309	1,938	913	448	5,390	2,677	2,713
Nevada	8	1,975	1,124	561	204	127	1,752	719	1,033
New Hampshire	80	1,643	1,029	395	174	139	1,412	572	840
New Jersey	221	23,304	12,677	7,243	2,594	1,710	20,352	8,479	11,873
New Mexico	73	2,848	1,535	906	421	202	2,485	1,076	1,409
New York [1]	276	149,722	86,170	26,745	28,607	10,845	115,065	63,063	51,992
North Carolina	89	14,064	7,642	3,672	2,190	966	11,645	5,400	6,245
North Dakota	167	2,293	1,138	899	210	163	2,039	836	1,203
Ohio	496	34,106	18,194	10,612	4,171	2,658	28,274	11,352	16,921
Oklahoma	447	9,694	4,737	3,214	1,438	728	8,269	3,956	4,314
Oregon	44	6,637	3,647	1,775	873	466	5,479	2,275	3,204
Pennsylvania	415	49,299	28,281	13,505	5,748	3,731	39,711	15,852	23,869
Rhode Island	14	2,856	1,893	614	244	205	2,391	880	1,511
South Carolina	91	4,373	2,367	1,225	641	330	3,720	2,224	1,496
South Dakota	159	2,639	1,414	889	279	185	2,368	907	1,461
Tennessee	317	13,928	7,601	3,879	1,894	956	11,691	4,994	6,696
Texas	1,269	46,862	22,940	14,447	7,811	3,211	38,557	19,943	18,614
Utah	53	3,170	1,809	726	825	221	2,708	1,208	1,500
Vermont	38	1,345	896	299	118	97	1,210	373	837
Virginia	271	14,606	8,751	3,656	1,681	983	12,241	4,860	7,381
Washington	85	9,726	5,317	2,578	1,396	574	7,668	3,355	4,313
West Virginia	210	5,211	2,642	2,016	505	418	4,362	1,704	2,658
Wisconsin	616	15,250	8,746	4,490	1,509	1,042	13,094	4,752	8,342
Wyoming	71	1,440	739	467	191	108	1,268	528	741
Puerto Rico [1]	9	4,722	3,008	688	563	224	3,470	1,269	2,202
Guam and American Samoa [3]	1	446	234	1	79	2	426	89	337
Virgin Islands [4]	2	410	291	30	32	9	366	114	251

[1] Includes data for 17 insured branches operated by 3 State nonmember banks in Puerto Rico.

[2] Includes data for 22 insured branches operated by 2 national banks in New York.

[3] Consists of data for 14 insured branches located in Guam operated by 1 national bank in California, 2 national banks in New York, and 2 State nonmember banks located in Hawaii; and includes data for 1 insured branch located in American Samoa operated by 1 State nonmember bank in Hawaii.

[4] Includes data for 21 insured branches operated by 2 national banks in New York, 1 national bank in California, and 2 State member banks in Pennsylvania.

Source: U.S. Federal Deposit Insurance Corporation, *Assets and Liabilities: Commercial and Mutual Savings Banks*, semiannual.

4. Changes in Commercial Banking Structure: 1953 to 1973 [Minus sign (—) denotes decrease]

CHANGE	1953–1973	1959 and 1960	1961 and 1962	1963 and 1964	1965 and 1966	1967 and 1968	1969 and 1970	1971 and 1972	1973
ALL COMMERCIAL BANKS									
Number of banks, beginning of period	14,074	13,527	13,471	13,428	13,760	13,766	13,678	13,687	13,936
New banks organized	3,382	248	295	635	317	197	819	469	343
Mergers and absorptions	3,118	298	322	288	286	266	297	208	87
Voluntary liquidations and suspensions	149	6	18	13	25	19	13	12	3
Number of banks, end of period	14,189	13,471	13,428	13,760	13,766	13,678	13,687	13,936	14,189
Net change	115	—56	—45	334	6	—88	9	249	253
STATES WITH STATEWIDE BRANCH BANKING [1]									
Number of banks, beginning of period	1,865	1,602	1,533	1,485	1,537	1,479	1,394	1,306	1,341
New banks organized	667	36	58	152	50	32	42	106	90
Mergers and absorptions	1,116	105	106	98	107	115	129	71	35
Voluntary liquidations and suspensions	10	-	-	2	1	2	1	1	-
Number of banks, end of period	1,396	1,533	1,485	1,537	1,479	1,394	1,306	1,341	1,396
Net change	—459	—69	—48	52	—58	—85	—88	35	55
STATES WITH LIMITED BRANCH BANKING [2]									
Number of banks, beginning of period	5,064	5,433	5,319	5,184	5,123	5,058	4,995	4,941	4,902
New banks organized	828	57	67	115	102	76	99	99	74
Mergers and absorptions	1,796	169	196	173	155	130	149	133	47
Voluntary liquidations and suspensions	58	2	6	3	12	9	4	5	1
Number of banks, end of period	4,928	5,319	5,184	5,123	5,058	4,995	4,941	4,902	4,928
Net change	—1,026	—114	—135	—61	—65	—63	—54	—39	26
STATES WITH UNIT BANKING [3]									
Number of banks, beginning of period	6,265	6,492	6,619	6,757	7,100	7,229	7,289	7,440	7,693
New banks organized	1,887	155	170	368	165	89	178	264	179
Mergers and absorptions	206	24	20	17	24	21	19	4	5
Voluntary liquidations and suspensions	81	4	12	8	12	8	8	7	2
Number of banks, end of period	7,865	6,619	6,757	7,100	7,229	7,289	7,440	7,693	7,865
Net change	1,600	127	138	343	129	60	151	253	172

- Represents zero. [1] Alaska, Ariz., Calif., Conn., Del., Hawaii, Idaho, Maine, Md., Nev., N.J., N.C., Oreg., R.I., S.C., S. Dak., Utah, Vt., Va., Wash., and D.C. [2] Limited usually to county where bank's head office is located or to contiguous counties: Ala., Ga., Ind., Ky., La., Mass., Mich., Miss., N.H., N. Mex., N.Y., Ohio, Pa., Tenn., and Wis. [3] Branch banking strictly limited or prohibited: Ark., Colo., Fla., Ill., Iowa, Kans., Minn., Mo., Mont., Nebr., N. Dak., Okla., Tex., W. Va., and Wyo.

Source of tables: Board of Governors of the Federal Reserve System, *Federal Reserve Bulletin*, and unpublished data.

5. LARGEST COMMERCIAL BANKS—FINANCIAL DATA, BY RANK OF ASSETS: 1960 to 1973

[In billions of dollars, except percent. As of December 31]

ASSET GROUP	1960		1965		1970		1973	
	Assets	Deposits	Assets	Deposits	Assets	Deposits	Assets	Deposits
50 largest	98.6	85.5	146.7	124.6	220.0	173.9	311.6	239.2
Percent of all commercial banks	39.1	38.5	39.4	38.4	34.3	32.2	33.6	31.3
Lowest ten	6.6	5.9	9.2	8.1	16.4	13.5	23.2	18.9
Second ten	8.1	7.2	12.1	10.6	19.5	16.4	27.7	21.3
Third ten	10.4	9.3	14.8	12.9	24.2	20.0	33.3	26.6
Fourth ten	19.3	16.8	28.9	24.8	42.4	33.6	60.7	45.1
Highest ten	54.3	46.4	81.7	68.1	117.4	90.5	166.7	127.4
Percent of total	100.0	100.0	100.0	100.0	100.0	100.0	100.0	100.0
Lowest ten	6.6	6.8	6.3	6.5	7.4	7.7	7.4	7.9
Second ten	8.2	8.4	8.2	8.5	8.9	9.4	8.9	8.9
Third ten	10.6	10.9	10.1	10.4	11.0	11.5	10.7	11.1
Fourth ten	19.5	19.6	19.7	19.9	19.3	19.3	19.5	18.8
Highest ten	55.0	54.3	55.7	54.7	53.4	52.0	53.5	53.2

Source: U.S. Federal Deposit Insurance Corporation, unpublished data.

Appendix D

THRIFT INSTITUTIONS

Source: Statistical Abstract of the United States, 1974; Department of Commerce, Social and Economic Statistics Administration, Bureau of the Census, pp. 455, 457.

1. MUTUAL SAVINGS BANKS—ASSETS, LIABILITIES, AND SURPLUS ACCOUNTS: 1950 TO 1973

[Money figures in millions of dollars. As of Dec. 31. Includes Puerto Rico and Virgin Islands. See *Historical Statistics, Colonial Times to 1957*, series N 155 and X 95-96, for related data]

ITEM	1950	1955	1960	1965	1970	1971	1972	1973
Number of banks	529	528	515	506	494	490	486	482
Assets	**22,385**	**31,271**	**40,574**	**58,220**	**79,227**	**89,573**	**100,599**	**106,660**
Loans and discounts, net [1]	8,137	17,457	27,122	15,280	60,353	64,186	70,593	77,096
Real estate loans	8,261	17,457	26,935	41,617	2 57,948	2 61,978	67,556	73,230
All other loans	128	213	418	894		2,208	3,037	3,866
Securities	13,209	12,442	11,992	10,971	16,199	21,684	26,254	25,232
U.S. Government obligations, direct and guaranteed	10,868	8,460	6,239	5,470	4,976	6,267	7,588	6,994
Fed. securities, not guaranteed	2,072	2,690	4,251	846	11,223	15,417	18,666	18,238
Other securities	269	1,292	1,501	4,656	2,674	3,703	3,752	4,332
Other assets	1,039	1,375	1,460	1,059				
Liabilities and surplus accounts	**22,385**	**31,271**	**40,574**	**58,220**	**79,227**	**89,573**	**100,599**	**106,660**
Deposits	20,031	28,182	36,353	52,761	72,086	81,978	92,225	97,166
Miscellaneous liabilities	106	257	669	745	1,217	1,266	1,413	1,902
Surplus accounts	2,247	2,812	3,553	4,663	5,924	6,328	6,961	7,592

[1] Beginning 1970, data on gross basis and not comparable with earlier years. [2] Includes valuation reserves.

Source: U.S. Federal Deposit Insurance Corporation, *Annual Report*.

2. FEDERAL AND STATE-CHARTERED CREDIT UNIONS—SUMMARY: 1950 TO 1973

[As of December 31. Includes District of Columbia, Puerto Rico, Canal Zone, Guam, and Virgin Islands, except as noted. See also *Historical Statistics, Colonial Times to 1957*, series X 403-414]

YEAR	Credit unions reporting [1]		Members (1,000)		Assets (mil. dol.)		Loans out-standing (mil. dol.)		Savings (mil. dol.)	
	Federal	State [2]	Federal	State [2]	Federal	State [2]	Federal	State [2]	Federal	State [2][3]
1950	4,984	5,587	2,127	2,483	406	600	264	416	362	522
1960	9,905	10,151	6,087	5,971	2,670	2,989	2,021	2,381	2,344	2,637
1965	11,543	10,521	8,641	8,115	5,166	5,385	3,865	4,233	4,538	4,682
1970	12,977	10,679	11,966	10,853	8,861	9,089	6,069	7,137	7,629	7,894
1971	12,717	10,536	12,702	11,382	10,553	10,569	8,071	8,081	9,191	9,167
1972	12,708	10,354	13,572	12,118	12,514	12,275	9,424	9,239	10,956	9,622
1973 (prel.)	12,732	10,270	14,626	13,072	14,535	14,019	11,007	10,726	12,575	12,028

[1] Does not represent total number chartered; reports are not received from all credit unions in operation, and some are inactive. However, the number of Federal unions reporting is same as number in operation.   [2] Alaska, Delaware, Hawaii, Nevada, South Dakota, Wyoming, Canal Zone, Guam, Virgin Islands, and, beginning 1965, District of Columbia have no State or local credit union law.   [3] Includes members' deposits.

Source: 1950-1965, U.S. Social Security Administration, *Federal Credit Union Program*, annual. Beginning 1970, National Credit Union Administration, *Annual Report of the Administrator* and *State-Chartered Credit Unions*.

3.

SAVINGS AND LOAN ASSOCIATIONS—FINANCIAL ITEMS: 1950 TO 1973

[Money figures in billions of dollars. As of December 31, except as indicated. Includes Puerto Rico and Guam. See headnote, table 736. Beginning 1965, excludes associations which have either liquidated or converted to banks; for details, see source. See also *Historical Statistics, Colonial Times to 1957*, series N 196–203]

ITEM	1950	1955	1960	1965	1969	1970	1971	1972	1973 (prel.)
Number of associations	6.0	6.1	6.3	6.2	5.8	5.7	5.5	5.3	5.2
Total assets	16.9	37.7	71.5	129.6	162.1	176.2	206.0	243.1	272.4
Cash and investment securities	2.5	4.5	7.9	12.1	13.8	16.5	21.0	24.4	21.0
Mortgage loans outstanding [1]	13.7	31.4	60.1	110.3	140.2	150.3	174.3	206.2	232.1
FHA and VA	3.8	7.3	10.7	11.5	15.6	18.7	24.3	28.9	29.7
Conventional	9.8	24.1	49.3	98.8	124.7	131.7	150.0	177.3	202.4
Other assets	.8	1.7	3.5	7.2	8.1	9.3	10.7	12.6	19.2
Total liabilities	15.6	35.1	66.5	120.9	150.5	163.8	192.4	227.9	255.3
Savings capital	14.0	32.1	62.1	110.4	135.5	146.4	174.2	206.8	227.3
Other [2]	1.6	3.0	4.4	10.5	15.0	17.4	18.2	21.1	28.0
Net worth [2]	(NA)	(NA)	(NA)	(NA)	11.6	12.4	13.6	15.2	17.1
Mortgage loans made during year [1][3]	5.2	11.3	14.3	24.2	21.8	21.4	39.4	51.4	49.5
Home construction	1.8	4.0	4.7	6.0	4.8	4.2	6.8	8.5	8.4
Home purchase	2.2	5.2	6.1	10.8	11.3	10.2	18.8	26.6	28.2

NA Not available.

[1] Beginning 1969, real estate sold on contract included in mortgage lending data; prior years, in "Other assets." [2] Prior to 1970, permanent stock included in "Other liabilities"; thereafter, in "Net worth." [3] Includes loans not shown separately.

Source: U.S. Federal Home Loan Bank Board, *Savings and Home Financing Source Book*, annual, and unpublished data.

4. ALL SAVINGS AND LOAN ASSOCIATIONS—SELECTED FINANCIAL ITEMS, STATES AND OTHER AREAS: 1971

[Money figures in millions of dollars. As of December 31. Major balance sheet items for all operating and insured associations not identical with those shown in table 735, primarily because some State-chartered associations submit their reports on dates other than December 31]

STATE OR OTHER AREA	Number of associations	Total assets	Mortgage loans and contracts	Savings capital
Total	5,474	206,018	174,392	174,188
Alabama	69	1,585	1,333	1,370
Alaska	3	113	93	86
Arizona	13	1,513	1,203	1,232
Arkansas	63	1,225	1,024	1,084
California	207	36,934	31,966	30,067
Colorado	61	2,860	2,455	2,244
Connecticut	35	1,840	1,546	1,560
Delaware	28	123	108	104
District of Columbia	20	2,924	2,551	2,455
Florida	132	12,146	10,085	10,589
Georgia	104	3,790	3,264	3,103
Hawaii	11	752	656	612
Idaho	11	365	317	312
Illinois	545	16,587	13,933	14,096
Indiana	189	4,321	3,631	3,821
Iowa	89	2,285	1,961	1,961
Kansas	95	2,535	2,192	2,098
Kentucky	138	2,191	1,871	1,932
Louisiana	106	2,651	2,224	2,314
Maine	27	297	228	228
Maryland	258	3,742	3,192	3,181
Massachusetts	190	4,548	3,847	3,855
Michigan	65	5,760	4,898	5,012
Minnesota	74	3,910	3,280	3,381
Mississippi	78	1,044	870	892
Missouri	133	5,220	4,444	4,491
Montana	16	333	287	291
Nebraska	46	1,654	1,379	1,318
Nevada	6	653	533	501
New Hampshire	22	434	374	368
New Jersey	314	8,110	6,812	7,067
New Mexico	35	624	507	542
New York	187	12,667	10,667	10,061
North Carolina	185	4,075	3,519	3,547
North Dakota	14	695	494	494
Ohio	476	15,487	12,675	13,211
Oklahoma	59	1,823	1,570	1,677
Oregon	30	1,919	1,592	1,519
Pennsylvania	533	9,558	8,185	8,020
Rhode Island	7	467	391	400
South Carolina	73	2,049	1,749	1,761
South Dakota	19	289	245	257
Tennessee	71	2,358	1,969	2,061
Texas	277	9,182	7,696	7,703
Utah	17	1,024	891	800
Vermont	7	106	92	94
Virginia	75	2,410	2,071	2,110
Washington	58	3,169	2,666	2,716
West Virginia	37	512	426	452
Wisconsin	133	4,558	3,915	3,816
Wyoming	12	214	182	186
Puerto Rico	9	507	435	389
Guam	1	6	5	5

Source: U.S. Federal Home Loan Bank Board, Trends in the Savings and Loan Field, annual.

Appendix E   CONSUMER CREDIT

Source: Statistical Abstract of the United States, 1974; Department of Commerce, Social and Economic Statistics Administration, Bureau of the Census, p.461.

1.

CONSUMER CREDIT: 1950 TO 1974

[In billions of dollars, except percent. Prior to 1960, excludes Alaska and Hawaii. Estimated amounts of credit outstanding as of end of year or month; extended and repaid, for entire year or month. See also *Historical Statistics, Colonial Times to 1967*, series X 415–422]

TYPE OF CREDIT	1950	1955	1960	1965	1968	1969	1970	1971	1972	1973	1974 Mar.
Credit outstanding	21.5	38.8	56.1	89.9	110.8	121.1	127.2	138.4	157.6	180.5	177.6
Ratio to disposable personal income [1] percent	10.4	14.1	16.0	19.0	18.7	19.1	18.4	18.6	19.8	20.5	19.1
Installment	14.7	28.9	43.0	70.9	87.7	97.1	102.1	111.3	127.3	147.3	145.8
Automobile paper	6.1	13.5	17.7	28.4	32.9	35.5	35.2	38.7	44.1	51.1	50.3
Other consumer goods paper	4.8	7.6	11.5	18.5	24.6	28.3	31.5	34.4	40.1	47.5	46.5
Home improvement loans [2]	1.0	1.7	3.7	3.7	4.2	4.6	5.1	5.4	6.2	7.4	7.4
Personal loans	2.8	6.1	10.6	20.2	25.9	28.7	30.3	32.9	36.9	41.4	41.5
Noninstallment	6.8	9.9	13.2	19.0	23.0	24.0	25.1	27.1	30.2	33.0	31.8
Single-payment loans	1.8	3.0	4.5	7.7	9.5	9.7	9.7	10.6	12.3	13.2	13.2
Charge accounts	3.4	4.8	5.3	6.4	7.2	7.4	8.0	8.4	9.0	9.8	7.9
Service credit	1.6	2.1	3.3	4.9	6.3	6.9	7.5	8.2	9.0	10.0	10.7
Installment credit:											
Extended	21.6	39.0	50.0	78.7	100.0	109.1	112.2	124.3	143.0	165.1	13.2
Repaid	18.4	33.6	46.1	70.5	91.7	99.8	107.2	115.1	126.9	145.0	13.4
Net change	3.1	5.3	3.7	8.2	8.3	9.4	5.0	9.2	16.0	20.1	-0.2
Policy loans by life insurance companies [3]	2.4	3.3	5.2	7.7	11.3	13.8	16.1	17.1	18.0	(NA)	(NA)
Delinquency rate, 30 days and over, percent of installment debt [4]	2.20	1.59	1.93	1.81	1.82	1.98	2.14	1.93	2.19	2.53	[5] 2.70

[1] For disposable-personal income figures used to derive these data, see table 600.
[2] Holdings of financial institutions; holdings of retail outlets are included in "Other consumer goods paper."
[3] Source: Institute of Life Insurance, New York, N.Y. Year end figures are annual statement asset values; month end figures are book value of ledger assets. These loans are excluded in consumer credit series.
[4] Source: American Bankers Association, New York, N.Y. Seasonal adjustments by U.S. Bureau of Economic Analysis.   [5] Feb. data.

111

2. CONSUMER INSTALLMENT CREDIT OUTSTANDING, BY HOLDER: 1950 TO 1974

[In billions of dollars. As of end of year or month. Prior to 1960, excludes Alaska and Hawaii. Estimated]

HOLDER	1950	1955	1960	1965	1968	1969	1970	1971	1972	1973	1974 Mar.
Total	14.7	28.9	43.0	70.9	87.7	97.1	102.1	111.3	127.3	1 147.4	145.8
Financial institutions	11.8	24.4	36.7	61.1	75.7	84.0	88.2	97.1	111.4	129.3	128.8
Commercial banks	5.8	10.6	16.7	29.0	37.9	42.4	45.4	51.2	59.8	69.5	69.2
Finance companies	5.3	11.8	15.4	23.9	26.1	27.8	27.7	28.9	32.1	37.2	37.0
Credit unions	.6	1.7	3.9	7.3	10.3	12.0	13.0	14.8	16.9	19.6	19.6
Miscellaneous lenders ¹	.1	.3	.6	1.0	1.4	1.7	2.1	2.3	2.6	3.0	3.0
Retail outlets	2.9	4.5	6.3	9.8	12.0	13.1	13.9	14.2	16.0	18.1	17.0

¹ ⁻ cludes savings and loan associations and mutual savings banks.

Source of tables: Except as noted, Board of Governors of the Federal Reserve System, *Federal Reserve Bulletin*, monthly.

3.

CREDIT-CARD BANKING, BY CLASS OF BANK: 1967 TO 1973

[Covers insured commercial banks offering credit-card plans]

ITEM	Dec. 31, 1967	Dec. 31, 1968	Dec. 31, 1969	Dec. 31, 1970	Dec. 31, 1971	June 30, 1972	Dec. 31, 1972	June 30, 1973	Dec. 31, 1973
All banks.........number..	390	510	1,207	1,432	1,535	1,588	1,631	1,699	1,765
Amount outstanding......mill. dol..	828	1,312	2,639	3,792	4,490	4,562	5,408	5,609	6,838
National banks.......number..	187	272	618	704	766	780	801	819	840
Amount outstanding......mill. dol..	636	1,019	1,960	2,727	3,250	3,308	3,931	4,006	4,999
State member banks......number..	50	65	155	175	187	184	182	187	191
Amount outstanding......mill. dol..	145	210	470	709	835	837	966	1,058	1,192
Nonmember banks.......number..	153	173	434	553	582	624	648	693	734
Amount outstanding......mill. dol..	47	83	209	356	405	417	511	545	647
Accounts with outstanding balances, number........1,000..	(NA)	(NA)	17,500	¹ 16,441	19,450	(NA)	20,586	(NA)	(NA)

NA Not available.   ¹ Excludes nonmember banks.

Source: Board of Governors of the Federal Reserve System, *Bank Credit-Card and Check-Credit Plans,* July 1968; *Federal Reserve Bulletin,* June 1972, *Report of Condition of Domestic Commercial Banks,* September 1973; and unpublished data.

Appendix F

BANK SUSPENSIONS

Source: Statistical Abstract of the United States, 1974; Department of Commerce, Social and Economic Statistics Administration, Bureau of the Census, p. 452.

1. BANK SUSPENSIONS—NUMBER OF BANKS AND AMOUNT OF DEPOSITS: 1930 TO 1973

[Prior to 1959, excludes Alaska and Hawaii. Banks closed either permanently or temporarily, on account of financial difficulties, by order of supervisory authorities or by directors of banks. "Member," refers to membership in Federal Reserve System. All national banks are Federal Reserve System member; all Federal Reserve System members are insured. See also *Historical Statistics, Colonial Times to 1957*, series X 165–178]

YEAR OR PERIOD	NUMBER OF BANKS					DEPOSITS (mil. dol.)				
	Total	National	State member	Nonin-sured	In-sured	Total	National	State member	Nonin-sured	In-sured
1930	1,352	161	27	1,164	(X)	853	170	202	481	(X)
1931	2,294	409	107	1,778	(X)	1,691	489	294	958	(X)
1932	1,456	276	55	1,125	(X)	716	214	55	446	(X)
1933	4,004	1,101	174	2,729	(X)	8,699	1,611	783	1,205	(X)
1934–1940	313	16	6	84	207	182	15	27	41	50
1941–1946	22	6	-	4	12	12	8	-	(Z)	4
1947–1950	6	-	-	6	-	3	-	-	8	-
1951–1955	17	2	1	7	7	68	5	19	5	20
1956–1960	19	3	1	8	7	41	18	1	6	10
1961–1965	28	5	1	11	11	99	48	2	-	43
1966–1970	10	4	2	-	4	35	24	5	-	6
1970	1	1	-	-	-	15	15	-	-	-
1971	3	1	-	-	2	6	1	-	-	-
1972	2	1	-	1	1	57	-	-	36	4
1973	3	-	-	1	3	21	-	-	-	21

- Represents zero.   X Not applicable.   Z Less than $500,000.

114

2.

Source: Code of Federal Regulations, Vol. 12, Banks and Banking,

PART 305--PAYMENT OF INSURED DEPOSITS

§ 305.1 Payment of insured deposits in closed banks.

When an insured bank closes under circumstances requiring the Corporation to make payment of the insured deposits[1] therein, as prescribed by law,[2] the Board of Directors appoints one or more Claim Agents with power and authority as provided by law[3] who maintain a temporary office at the site of the closed bank for the purpose of receiving claims for insured deposits and making payment thereof as soon as possible in accordance with applicable law. Claimants for insured deposits are required to submit to such Claim Agents appropriate proofs of claim, in form and manner prescribed by law or by the Board of Directors to deliver up any pass book or other record issued by the bank evidencing the insured deposit, to assign their claims for insured deposits to the Corporation to the extent required by law, and to furnish proper identification. The claimant is required to make proof thereof to the satisfaction of the Claim Agent. Disputed claims which cannot be adjusted in the field are referred to the Chief of the Division of Liquidation for determination and when satisfactory disposition cannot be so made, may be referred to the Board of Directors for appropriate action. In cases where the Corporation is not satisfied as to the validity of a claim for an insured deposit, it may require the final determination of a court of competent jurisdiction before paying such claim. The Corporation is authorized to make payment of the insured deposits in cash or by making available to each depositor a transferred deposit in a "new bank,"[4] which is insured, in the same community or in another insured bank in an amount equal to the insured deposit of such depositor. Any such transferred deposit would be a demand deposit in the absence of an agreement between the depositor and

---

[1] Defined in section 3(m) of the Federal Deposit Insurance Act.

[2] See section 11 of the Federal Deposit Insurance Act, particularly subsections (b), (f) and (g).

[3] See section 10(b) of the Federal Deposit Insurance Act.

[4] See section 11(h)-(1) of the Federal Deposit Insurance Act, 12 U.S.C. 1821 (h)-(1).

transferee bank providing for a time or savings deposit. It is the policy of the Corporation to make such payment by issuing its check for the amount of the insured deposit. In making such payments, the Corporation exercises its statutory authority to withhold payment of such portion of the insured deposit of any depositor as may be required to provide for the payment of any liability of such depositor as a stockholder of the bank, or of any liability of such depositor to the closed bank or its receiver, which is not offset against a claim due from the bank, pending the determination and payment of such liability by the depositor or any other person liable therefor.

(Sec. 9, 64 Stat. 881; 12 U.S.C. 1819) [15 F.R. 8632, Dec. 6, 1950, as amended at 19 F.R. 1666, Mar. 27, 1954; 32 F.R. 9638, July 4, 1967]

Appendix G

BOUNDARIES OF FEDERAL RESERVE DISTRICTS

DATE DUE